After Mormonism, What?

Books by Latayne C. Scott

The Mormon Mirage
Open Up Your Life: A Woman's Workshop on Hospitality
To Love Each Other: A Woman's Workshop on First Corinthians 13
*Time, Talents, Things: A Woman's Workshop on Christian
    Stewardship*
Crisis: Crucible of Praise
Why We Left Mormonism: Eight People Tell Their Stories
A Marriage Made in Heaven
Why We Left a Cult: Six People Tell Their Stories

After Mormonism, What?

Reclaiming the Ex-Mormon's Worldview for Christ

Latayne C. Scott

Baker Books

A Division of Baker Book House Co.
Grand Rapids, Michigan 49516

Published by Baker Books
a division of Baker Book House Company
P.O. Box 6287, Grand Rapids, MI 49516–6287

Printed in the United States of America

Library of Congress Cataloging-in-Publication Data

Scott, Latayne Colvett, 1952-
  After Mormonism, what? / Latayne C. Scott.
     p.   cm.
  Includes bibliographical references and indexes.
  ISBN 0-8010-8350-8
  1. Missions to Mormons. 2. Converts. Protestant—Religious life. 3. Mormon Church—Controversial literature. 4. Church of Jesus Christ of Latter-Day Saints—Controversial literature. I. Title.
BV2627.S36   1993
248.2'4—dc20   93–10784

For my dear mother
Rose Hensley

Reclaim: 1. to rescue or bring back (someone) from error, vice, etc. 2. to make (desert, etc.) capable of being cultivated or lived in, as by irrigating, etc. 3. to obtain (useful material, etc.) from waste products.

—*Webster's New World Dictionary of the American Language*

Contents

Part 1

The Territory

Here is my servant, whom I uphold,
   my chosen one in whom I delight;
I will put my Spirit on him
   and he will bring justice to the nations.
He will not shout or cry out,
   or raise his voice in the streets.
A bruised reed he will not break,
   and a smoldering wick he will not snuff out.
In faithfulness he will bring forth justice;
   he will not falter or be discouraged
till he establishes justice on earth.
   In his law the islands will put their hope.

                   —Isaiah 42:1–4

I tell you, open your eyes and look at the fields! They are ripe for harvest.

                   —John 4:35

Why This Book?

Unless God directs otherwise, this will be the last book I write about Mormonism.

For years I have marveled at the way my first book, *The Mormon Mirage* (Zondervan, 1979), came into being. I was put into contact (providentially, I believe) with a famous Christian author who, when she learned that I was both a writer and an ex-Mormon, asked, "Why haven't you written about your experiences?" She put me in touch with Zondervan, a Christian publishing company, which at enormous potential risk published a book by me, an unknown author. It quixotically took on the multibillion-dollar theological empire of Mormonism. That book was written during a once-in-a-lifetime epoch, when my doctrinal solidity and emotional distance from Mormonism were exactly balanced against the clarity with which I remembered my experiences in Mormonism. I could not have written the book earlier, because I was too close to Mormonism; and I could not have written it later, because I was too far from Mormonism.

My second book on Mormonism likewise came about in a way which convinced me that it was God's will, not just mine. I was contacted by Baker Book House's acquisitions editor, who asked me to write about my experiences and those of others who had left Mormonism in such a way as to offer practical help to those leaving.

In my first book I was very open about how Mormonism made me feel. In my second I was very open about how my leaving Mormonism made me feel. In this third book, I want to share what I have heretofore been most reluctant to address: what worked and did not work with me and with others I know in the long and painful process of learning Christian doctrine and living.

Part of my reluctance to write such a book as this was because I did not want to address in such a public way some of the mistakes made by those Christian individuals who discipled me. You see, I don't want to be guilty of the sin of ingratitude, and I have no desire to criticize the people who made a decision to love and accept me even though I was a bundle of raw emotions, mistrust, and skewed doctrinal conceptions. They addressed the only needs they knew I had, emotional needs to be loved in spite of my difference from them. Except for a two-and-one-half year period when our family lived in Colorado, I have willingly worshiped with the same group of people for almost twenty years. Obviously they do something right to make me want to stay with them this long.

On the other hand, when I first became a Christian, there was not among them one person who was familiar with Mormon doctrine or who could identify with my feelings about having been a member of a cult. It was five years after my conversion to Christianity that I met my first ex-Mormon Christian, five very lonely years that at times seemed to be the fulfillment of the complete aloneness that more than one Mormon had predicted would be the result of my leaving that church.

In the meantime, my fellow Christians acted on the only information they had about Mormonism—that Mormons were clean-living, hard-working people with a real sense of loyalty and community—and they accepted me as such. (They assumed the best about me—not a bad rule of thumb.) They took for granted that I had given up loyalty to Salt Lake leadership, the *Book of Mormon*, polygamy, and the Word of Wisdom. They also took for granted that I relied only on the Bible for doctrine and was loyal to them as a group of people. They thought that I should, with those two supports, be able to make "Christian" decisions. But no one sat down with me and addressed my deep needs for spiritual nurture.

Nobody gave me instruction on how to use the Bible for study and meditation and as a guide for life, not just for proof texts as I had been taught to do. Nobody gave me guidance on how to know God or even to figure out who he was.

Now, I cannot fault them for not meeting needs that even I didn't know I had. You see, I believed as they did that just giving up the extrabiblical things about Mormonism would make me a Christian. But neither they nor I knew what those things were. Most of us think that going from one belief system to another is like emptying out a bucket, then refilling it with new information. The trouble is that none of us can or want to completely empty our minds. Instead, we replace one concept with another. Meanwhile, all the old, erroneous concepts remain until we identify them as erroneous and then replace them.

An example of this occurred some six months after I became a Christian. I was sitting in a Sunday school class where the Bible text under discussion was Colossians 1:15: "He [Jesus] is the image of the invisible God." I raised my hand to answer the teacher's question about what that meant by saying, "Well, that means that God has a physical body that looks very much like that of Jesus."

There was a great deal of muttering, and I knew I'd said something wrong, but unfortunately no one came to me and said, "You know, I'd love to meet you for a cup of coffee and share some Scripture with you about God and what the word *image* means here in Colossians and elsewhere in the New Testament."

Maybe that was because my brothers and sisters who knew something about Mormonism were overwhelmed with the prospect of trying to "unlearn" me of so much error. Maybe it was because they assumed that this was my husband's job. (He should have known what he was getting into when he married me, right?) Or maybe some of them weren't exactly sure why they believed what they did about God; they only were certain they must be right (and since they'd gotten that confidence somewhat osmotically, if I just stuck around for a while, I'd feel the same way soon enough). At any rate, the job did not get done, and I lived for years with great uncertainty about the identities of God, Jesus Christ, and the Holy Spirit, and about other doctrinal matters of great import.

I know that this situation was not unique to me. An ex-Mormon friend of mine, Margaret Marshall of England, tells of how this happened in her own life.

"When I became a Christian," Margaret wrote in a letter to me, "I entered the Christian fold with many elements of Mormonism still in me. I knew the doctrines were false; however, I never sat down and used Scripture to verify this. . . . I feel sure God was aware that there were still many elements of Mormon doctrine still embedded in my heart." She went on to tell how after attending a Christian church for ten years, she was contacted by Mormon missionaries.

"I didn't know Scripture well enough to refute what they presented to me," Margaret wrote. As a result, she made a preliminary commitment for rebaptism into Mormonism. It was only some step-by-step contrasting of Mormon doctrine to biblical truth that helped her break that date with hell. She realizes now that her education as a Christian is a task she can no longer postpone.

Another problem I faced as a young Christian was the fact that the very loving and accepting group of Christians with whom I worshiped worked hard, played hard, fellowshiped hard, and didn't truck much with intangibles like piety and transcendence. For years, I believed that my hyperawareness of the presence of God and former practices of fasting and extended prayer were things that just did not fit into this new, "practical" lifestyle. Now I realize, years later, that there were certainly people in my congregation who were deeply spiritual. But they were the quiet ones. Thus it was that I got the impression that spiritual things were simply vestiges from my past and signs of my own personal vulnerability to the thought forms of Mormonism. Perhaps I fell quickly into this misconception because I knew that the last time I had fallen in love with a god he had broken my heart. I wasn't ready to open myself up to that kind of hurt again.

Unless you are yourself an ex-Mormon, you probably don't know what kinds of needs your new Christian friend has after having left Mormonism. But you are reading this book because you want to know, and that's great!

However, reading this book can be one of the most costly things you will ever do, because if you read it and decide to make the kinds of changes in *your* life that will allow you to effectively nurture your friend, your own life may also be transformed.

What I ask you to do is evangelize your own mind as you evangelize your friend, to convert your own heart and open it more fully to a very supernatural God. I am asking you to evaluate and teach yourself as well by giving you tools that will be useless unless you understand them.

I write this book at a time when even my hurt of remembering my early years as a Christian is beginning to fade. It is my "final hurrah" in teaching people about what to do to help their ex-Mormon friends.

In a way, this is my last will and testament of my Mormon heritage. I bequeath to the body of Christ what I have learned.

1

The Problem, Illustrated:
The Collapse
of a Belief System

A long, handwritten letter arrived recently at my home. It was from a woman I have never met, who lives thousands of miles from me. She began by telling me she had just finished reading the first half of my book *The Mormon Mirage*, which tells of why and how I left the Mormon Church almost twenty years ago, and of her feelings of closeness to me after reading the book.

I have received hundreds of letters since 1979, when this book first appeared, and I am grateful for the interest shown in it. I try to answer each letter personally. But the depth and scope of emotion in a letter from a woman named Diane Johnston overwhelmed me.

"I left the church five years ago," she wrote. "Unfortunately, the church has not left me. Oh! I hurt so badly—still.

"I'm only halfway through your story and I *know* that all I had been taught was inaccurate and wrong. God let me

19

know that in no uncertain terms. I'm hurt. I'm angry, I'm empty—I'm nowhere.

"I've spent the past five years studying and praying and wondering. Sometimes things get so confused in my mind that I'm not sure if the information in my head is Mormon or non-Mormon. I'm just not *sure* of anything anymore. I'm afraid to be sure. That's a truth about myself that I came to realize while reading your book."

Diane's letter went on to tell in detail about her early life. Her father was a Navy career man, so her church background was "general Protestant chapel." But her father had a great interest in the Mormon Tabernacle Choir and listened often to broadcasts of their music (and, of course, the accompanying doctrinal lessons).

When Diane married, she married a "jack Mormon" who didn't practice the religion. But when their daughter Cathi was born prematurely and with what was diagnosed as terminal spinal meningitis, Diane's husband called a local Mormon bishop to bless the child.

Though doctors had said Cathi would not live through the night, within hours the child was greatly improved. The next day her fever was gone, and a spinal tap revealed absolutely no evidence of the disease.

"That was all the convincing I needed," Diane wrote. "Two weeks later I was baptized into the Mormon Church. I didn't even go through the lessons—I knew that a church whose members could accomplish a miracle like that just *had* to be true. What I failed to take into consideration at the time was the fact that the father of one of my friends (who was a pastor) had prayer groups outside my Cathi's room twenty-four hours a day.

"So, I was baptized and confirmed, and every time I looked at my daughter, I saw again the miracle of her complete healing with no side effects. This deepened my love for the church. What I realize now is that it should have been my love of *God* that deepened, not my love for the church."

During the ensuing twelve years, Diane held many leadership positions in her local ward. However, her efforts to get her husband to stop smoking so that he could qualify for a temple recommend and they could be "sealed" in eternal marriage were suddenly stymied by a shocking development in her life.

Her husband was accused of indecent exposure and molesting some of his daughter Cathi's friends. Both her husband and her bishop assured Diane that the charges were totally false.

"The bishop told us that since Satan was working so hard, we must be destined for some very good things, works in the future. As funny as it seems now, it made perfect sense at the time."

Diane was further reassured when her husband received his patriarchal blessing (viewed by Mormons as a very personalized message from God), which stated, "The angels of the Lord have been watching over you and you have done nothing on this earth to be ashamed of." Even their stake president, who also is supposed to be able to receive direct revelation about members, granted them a temple recommend.

After their temple marriage, Diane's husband was found guilty of the exposure and molestation charges. Church leaders told Diane and her husband that the conviction had taken place because they had "defied Satan" and gone through with the temple ceremonies. Her husband's conviction forced him out of the Air Force and into mandatory counseling. All the while, Diane battled and submerged her recurrent doubts about her husband's protestations of innocence.

In the coming years, her husband became more and more active in the church. He was called to be a counselor to his ward's bishop, and finally a bishop himself. Diane served as Relief Society president, Young Woman's president, and in other capacities. But her friends brought disquieting stories to her about how her husband had approached them in ways that made them very uncomfortable.

"Just hold true," her former bishop and stake president advised when she shared her growing doubts and evidence of her husband's infidelities. But she couldn't. She left him.

A month later he came to her house and made a shocking confession to her. He admitted that he had indeed molested their daughter Cathi's friends years before.

"He looked at me in a funny way and asked, 'Are you still going to be a member of the church?' I said, 'Of course.'"

It was hours later that the full implication of his confession struck her.

"The patriarch was wrong, the bishop was wrong, and the stake president was wrong! But how could they be wrong if they were in touch with God?"

The further ongoing implications devastated her.

"You know, I would go through ten divorces before going through the experience of losing my God and church again. It was the most agonizingly horrible day of my life . . . I couldn't believe that for eighteen years I had been praying to a God that didn't exist.

"I was convinced that if there was no God in the Mormon Church, then there was no God anywhere! I mean, if the LDS [Latter-day Saints] beliefs weren't true, there could be nothing else."

In the midst of all this turmoil Diane decided to get drunk. However, she was so inexperienced with liquor that she had to call a friend to find out how to do it. Perceptively, the friend, Dale, came to her house, comforted and counseled her, and helped her through this difficult time.

"He patiently started to help me rebuild my faith. I later married this man, Dale, and he's been a real rock for me to anchor to while I've been bouncing around in the terms of my belief.

"But you know, that was only the beginning," Diane's letter continued. She told of the pain that had filled her life in the five years since she left the Mormon Church. "If I had known about the agony that I sometimes go through, maybe

I would have thought twice about leaving the church. As you said in your story, if something as strong as my mores and values based on my church are wrong, how can I believe any others are true?

"It's so hard to let myself believe in something again. I feel like I'm going through a debriefing; I have to really struggle to accept any mores, values, or ideas from churches. It makes you feel very alone from everyone else in the world.

"I hate this feeling of deep betrayal and hurt. It seems to get in my way so often. How do you explain this to someone who's never been LDS? Where do you find former Saints to help you debrief?

"I know the LDS faith is not of God, so why do I have this urge, at times, to be back in?

"I can never go back, nor do I really want to. But, but, but. . . . I need to trust again.

"Does that come all of a sudden? Over a period of time?"

Elements of This Alienation

I don't remember exactly what I wrote to Diane when I responded to her letter other than to tell her that her feelings were normal, very similar to those of many, many others who had written to me or spoken with me about the traumatizing experience of leaving the Mormonism we had loved.

I wanted to assure her that Christ was worth all she had gone through, and that she would continue to find peace as she sought him. But her letter disturbed me deeply in a way that nothing had in a long, long, time, for it brought back in a painfully vivid way a lot of the emotions I had felt not only when I was in the process of leaving Mormonism but for years afterwards.

I was reminded of an odd fact that has stuck in my mind ever since I first heard it. Dr. Karen Horney, a pioneer in the field of psychology, was one of the first to diagnose and define a neurosis. She said that a neurosis is "lack of wholehearted-ness." I would not presume to diagnose anyone else's situa-tion, but I do know that my own feelings of divided loyalties, confusion, and near despair after I left Mormonism certainly fit the apostle James's description of the "double-minded" person, "blown and tossed by the wind" (James 1:6, 8).

The poignant questions in Diane's letter reached parts of me that are still tender to the touch, so to speak. And they made me remember all over again the conclusion I came to after I interviewed seven other ex-Mormons for my book *Why We Left Mormonism* (Baker Book House, 1990).

In that book I made the observation that people who leave Mormonism and become "newborns in Christ" are not the same type of spiritual babies as those who come to him from the world. They are not just newborns; they are born addicted and must be treated for and weaned away from their depen-dency (as well as be fed and nurtured like other babies).

Later, when I interviewed six people who had come to Christ out of cults (Jehovah's Witnesses, Christian Science, and the New Age movement) for my book *Why We Left a Cult* (Baker Book House, 1993), I observed that perhaps this analogy could be taken a step further. People who come out of cults to Christ are not just newborns who are born addicted, they are born addicted and bear the marks of the spiritual abuse they've suffered.

Consider the elements in Diane's letter that show the great difficulties faced by those who leave a group like Mormonism. Her letter is a road map of such emotions and contributing factors.

1. Feelings of aloneness and confusion. ("I'm empty—I'm nowhere . . . I get so confused in my mind that I'm not sure if the information in my head is Mormon or non-Mormon.")

2. Cultural acclimation that allowed the seeds of error to take root in a young mind. (Her father had made a point of having his family listen to LDS music and doctrinal televi-

sion and radio shows, paving the way for her to readily accept a Mormon man as her husband.)

3. The tendency to base feelings and opinions on personal experience in which the church got credit for beneficial results. (She based her faith in the church on the fact that her daughter had been healed after being blessed by a bishop instead of basing her faith on the alternative explanation of the prayer vigils of Christians. Additionally, her "human lived experience" took precedence over a desire to confirm reality through Scripture.)

4. A developing pattern of loyalty to experiences, people, and the organization instead of loyalty to God. ("It should have been my love for God that deepened, not my love for the church.")

5. Being urged not to leave the organization even when confronted with the truth that leaders are spiritually unreliable. (Her husband questioned her about leaving the church after he admitted that as her spiritual head he had lied to both her and his ecclesiastical superiors.)

6. A feeling that if faith in the LDS organization was gone, it would be impossible to have faith at all. ("If there was no God in the Mormon Church, then there was no God anywhere.")

7. Rebellion as a response to the destruction of faith. (She wanted to get drunk.)

8. Overwhelming and irrational desire to return to the comfort of the dogmatism of Mormonism. ("If I had known about the agony that I sometimes go through, maybe I would have thought twice about leaving the church.")

9. Growing lack of confidence in one's ability to make moral and doctrinal decisions alone. ("If something as strong as my mores and values based on my church are wrong, how can I believe any others are true?")

10. Trust as an issue: the inability to trust in anything again. ("It's so hard to let myself believe in something again.")

11. Suspicion of any organized religion. ("If the LDS beliefs weren't true, there could be nothing else.")

12. Increasing and profound alienation. ("I feel alone from everyone else in the world.")

13. The perception that while "regular" Christians may sympathize, they are unable to empathize with the ex-Mormon. ("How do you explain this to someone who's never been LDS?")

14. A need for personal contact with someone who has had a similar experience. ("Where do you find former Saints to help you debrief?")

The questions that Diane asked and the issues she raised are, I believe, typical of those feelings that most ex-Mormon Christians raise at a specific point in their spiritual development. Many of these questions simply disappear when the person decides to repent—the biblical word is *metanoia*—which involves a conviction that a previous way of life was sinful, and that it is not enough simply to turn away from it but that one must also commit oneself to God to complete the process. Jurgen Goetzmann, in the article on metanoia in the *Dictionary of New Testament Theology* (Colin Brown, ed., Zondervan, 1986, vol. 1, p. 359), shows the implications of this when he says, "God saves completely and finally, and thus man's conversion to God must be complete and final." Of course, Diane's letter is that of one who had not yet come to that point.

The Issue of Trust

At its root, the basic issue for an ex-Mormon Christian is trust, which has three elements.

First is to trust one's own perceptions about what is real. For Diane, her observation of her daughter's healing overrode any doubts she may otherwise have had about Mormon doctrine. Once she realized that her own ability to judge was faulty, even after she left the organization that fostered those misconceptions, she felt unable to trust her own ability to make decisions in the present and the future.

Second is to trust others. Of course, Diane's case of dealing over many years with a husband who was not only morally unfaithful but who marshaled church leadership to support him in his lies is extreme. But it also illustrates the feelings of most ex-Mormons who describe their situation as one in which they made themselves vulnerable and were then betrayed not only by individuals but by the church as an entity. This all but destroyed their ability to trust others.

Third is to recognize and trust God. The compromising of that trust is most tragic.

Where do you turn when you feel you can't trust yourself, others, or God?

Part 2

The Tools

I keep asking that the God of our Lord Jesus Christ, the glorious Father, may give you the Spirit of wisdom and revelation, so that you may know him better. I pray also that the eyes of your heart may be enlightened in order that you may know the hope to which he has called you, the riches of his glorious inheritance in the saints, and his incomparably great power for us who believe.

—Ephesians 1:17–19

2

Foundational Strategies

The apostle Paul asked the same basic questions that all the ex-Mormon Dianes of this world ask: What do you do when you feel you can't trust people, God, or your own perceptions about either? Paul asked the question this way: "How, then, can they call on the one they have not believed in?" (Rom. 10:14).

He answers that question with something we all know. He says that faith has only one basis: a Christ-centered message. That message must necessarily take different forms according to the audience who will receive it.

Some Basics

Before we get into methodologies, I want to lay some ground rules I believe are necessary for a Christian who is teaching a Mormon.

1. You as a Christian must be absolutely, uncompromisingly committed to Christ—more than you are committed

to your church, more than you are committed to your job, more than you are committed to any person or any heritage on this earth.

Many churchgoers do not have this commitment. An acquaintance of mine, who was raised in a fine Christian home and had attended church for the last fifteen years, recently "went off the deep end" into a worldly lifestyle after her divorce. Her Christian friends tried at various steps in her descent to convince her to return to church and to abandon her immoral behavior, but her brazenness and rebellion put great distance between them. At this point, one friend asked her gently, "What about Jesus?"

"I was loyal to the church itself and to the members," she replied. "But when they pulled away from me, I lost that loyalty. And as for Jesus—I never had a loyalty to him."

The point of this sad story is this caveat: Make sure that you convert the heart of an ex-Mormon to Jesus, not just to yourself or your church. I believe that "cultural Christianity" that is Christless will send as many people to hell as Mormonism will.

2. You must be willing to spend time in earnest and intimate prayer with God daily. If you are too busy to do this, then don't bother teaching someone else.

3. You must be committed to the Bible as the unassailable witness of truth on the earth. This commitment must be the result not only of a conscious decision but must have a basis in the fact that you are familiar with it.

This does not mean that you must be a graduate of a seminary or be trained in a formal way. It does mean that you must be determined to make your whole life "logos-centric." It means that if your study of the Bible has in the past been confined to group study of only certain passages or books of the Bible, you will repent and also resolve to read the Bible cover to cover over and over again for the rest of your life.

Reading the Bible in this way is very much like marriage. When you are dating, you only see certain aspects of a person. When you live with him or her day to day you can truly say, "I know this person."

Another wonderful benefit of reading the Bible as a message to humankind is that God will work through your dedicated reading and reveal astounding truths about himself and his ways. I have seen it over and over in my own life. Paul in Ephesians told readers that "in reading this, then, you will be able to understand my insight into the mystery of Christ" (3:4).

Now, there are two foundational principles about Scripture upon which a study with an ex-Mormon must be based. First is the inerrancy of Scripture. If you do not believe the Bible to be inerrant, you might find yourself agreeing with your ex-Mormon friend that it is unreliable and that there are mistakes in it, which will lead to a natural conclusion that there is a need for someone or something to correct those mistakes (as your friend was taught in Mormonism).

Closely related to the principle of inerrancy is the principle of harmony: the assumption that the Bible has no conflicting statements or doctrines. One very important help to understand passages that might at first glance seem to contradict each other is to remember a basic rule of Bible interpretation: Never use an obscure passage as a basis for explaining a clearer one. Work from the easy-to-understand passages about a particular concept to the less easily understood.

Your ex-Mormon friend will probably have some residual mistrust of the Bible, even if such mistrust is unconscious, because he or she has been taught that it contains errors and contradictions. Be prepared ahead of time—before you get to the stage of discussing the Bible as a specific topic—to answer questions about alleged contradictions. One book I have found helpful is Gleason Archer's *Encyclopedia of Bible Difficulties* (Zondervan, 1982). The format is questions and answers that resemble some of the questions about specific passages that might arise (John 10:34, for instance). Another good one is John Haley's *Alleged Discrepancies of the Bible* (Baker Book House, 1984).

4. You have to be willing to commit yourself to your ex-Mormon friend's life for at least a year. In several cases when I have helped with someone's conversion to Christ, I have told her, "I will give you a year of my life." During that year I would meet with her at least once a week just for individual Bible study and instruction in Christian life. I invited her to my home for social events and fellowship. I prayed for her daily. I made sure she attended church regularly. I encouraged her to look at all the events and circumstances of her former and present lives, as much as possible, from God's viewpoint.

Anyone reading this will immediately know that if you actively share your faith and lead people to Christ you cannot make such an intense commitment to every new convert. Whenever I have made a decision not to follow this way of nurturing a new Christian (either because of previous commitments, lack of time, or just my own selfishness), and no one else has stepped forward to do it, then the new convert either falls away or (at least at first) does not achieve a very high level of spiritual maturity. On the other hand, people who get this "newborn intensive care" stay close to the Lord. In my experience, even those who wander away from the Lord do not go very far, nor for very long.

There are no quick fixes for a thought system as pervasive and encompassing as Mormonism. You must be willing to go the distance, resist the urge to bail out, and rejoice in victory as your friend matures.

Now, if you are not already spending the time in prayer and Bible study that I have spoken of, then this can become the greatest year of your life, because in it you can begin to be the Christian you have always wanted to be. And besides the closeness to Christ and his Word that you will achieve, you will be able also to see and chart the spiritual growth in the life of another human being whom you are helping to become mature.

Think about it this way: In teaching and nurturing a new Christian, you "reproduce" yourself. As you evaluate yourself, ask, Do I want this new Christian to be like me? If not, this is a wonderful time to begin to make the changes in your own life and relationship with God you have always wanted. This will be a year you give not only to your ex-Mormon friend but to the Lord and to yourself.

The Bible contains a marvelous promise to those who teach others. In Philemon verse 6, Paul says that you can have *a full understanding* of every good thing you have in Christ as a result of being active in sharing your faith.

5. You must be able to recognize and transmit a knowledge of unseen realities to the new Christian. You can do that (as the chapters on symbolism will show you) through not only direct teaching of Scripture but also by helping make the new Christian aware of the invisible structures that literally support this world (as taught by the Book of Ephesians) and by helping him or her differentiate between what is worldly and practical and what is spiritual and compellingly real to a believer.

6. I strongly advise that you enter into this teaching venture with a partner. There are several reasons for this. First, an ex-Mormon Christian needs as many points of spiritual contact as possible. Second, two people in the training process double the manpower for the next task. Third, no one can predict the future. Circumstances may arise that may put you or your partner out of the picture and require that the remaining teacher take up the slack, either temporarily or permanently.

7. Heed the experienced advice of the late Dr. Walter Martin, who gave the following pointers in the *Christian Research Newsletter*. Though they were aimed at people who are teaching cult members, I believe they apply equally well to those who are teaching ex-cult members.

Identify with the cultist as a person and as a creation of God.

Labor persistently, "until *they* pull the plug."

Exhaust every effort to answer questions.

Allow the cultist to "save face" when he realizes that you may be right in your teaching. Appeal to him or her as a person of integrity, a fellow truth-seeker.

Don't approach a cultist with a spiritual chip on your shoulder.

Don't directly attack the founder of a cult.

Don't lose your patience, even when your student seems "dense."

8. "Let your gentleness be evident to all. The Lord is near" (Phil. 4:5).

The Strategy

With all these things as a foundation, I now offer you a "plan of attack" for teaching. These are its elements.

First, learn about the five elements that make up a person's worldview and apply this knowledge to your assessment of the presumptions that your Mormon friend has. The five elements of worldview are presented and discussed in following chapters.

Second, learn about the four secularly defined epistemologies, as well as the epistemology, or way of knowing, the Bible affords that is beyond just the knowing of facts. An illustration of this is symbolism, which, along with epistemologies, will be discussed in detail later.

Third, step by step compare LDS doctrines and Bible truths on the following subjects: the Godhead, the meaning of salvation and the nature of the church, the role of Scripture, how to trust other people, and the meaning of and limits to obedience.

Of course, you should recognize that the LDS doctrine you will be combating may not be what is written in its scriptures or doctrinal books. In fact, what your ex-Mormon friend believes may not align at all with many Mormon teachings of the past (because its doctrine changes) or with doctrine of the present (because your friend may not know or have fully accepted certain teachings). That is why I have included a set of questions for you to discuss with your friend so that you can assess what he or she believes and not spend a lot of time on "dead" issues. (For instance, many people who know almost nothing about Mormonism know the religion has been associated with polygamy. But trying to convince a contemporary Mormon not to practice it is a waste of time and misses the mark of what that Mormon needs to know.)

Fourth, learn how to ask questions that get to core issues with your ex-Mormon friend. One specific way this is achieved is to get him or her to define terms with you.

For instance, all doctrinally grounded Christians know that the issue of salvation is a vital one, so they jump right into a conversation with someone with a Mormon background by asking a question they consider to be crucial: "Are you sure you are saved?"

I remember as a young Mormon being accosted at a flea market by an earnest young evangelist who asked me that question. I could hardly contain my impatience at what I considered the superfluity and ignorance of the question. You see, Mormon doctrine says that the concept of salvation is just the ability to have one's body resurrected at the judgment. And since I believed that everyone would have his or her body raised, an urgent asking about it was just a waste of time. The real issue for me was whether or not I would be *exalted*. Whereas in Mormon doctrine salvation is universal, exaltation is the matter of where an individual will spend eternity—in which of the three degrees of glory Mormonism teaches comprise heaven.

So an essential rule of thumb in dealing with terminology is, *Don't assume anything.* Keep a notepad and pencil handy when you are teaching your ex-Mormon friend. Whenever you introduce a subject, write down your friend's definition of the terms you will discuss. You will soon discover in many cases that you may be using the same words in his or her vocabulary but with different definitions.

Now, all these ground rules may seem restrictive. I wish you would look at it differently. This chapter began with a description of the necessity of teaching found in Romans 10:14–15: "How, then, can they call on the one they have not believed in? And how can they believe in the one of whom they have not heard? And how can they hear without someone preaching to them? And how can they preach unless they are sent? As it is written, 'How beautiful are the feet of those who bring us good news!'"

Think of these guidelines and suggestions as a kind of anointing of your feet, the feet of someone who will bring to another soul the most precious gift of all—the good news of salvation.

3

Assessing
the Mormon Worldview

The God who made the world and everything in it is
the Lord of heaven and earth and does not live in
temples made by hands. And he is not served by
human hands, as if he needed anything, because he
himself gives all men life and breath and everything
else. From one man he made every nation of men,
that they should inhabit the whole earth; and he
determined the times set for them and the exact
places where they should live. God did this so that
men would seek him and perhaps reach out for him
and find him, though he is not far from each one of
us. For in him we live and move and have our being.
As some of your own poets have said, "We are his offspring."

Therefore since we are God's offspring, we should
not think that the divine being is like gold or silver or
stone—an image made by man's design and skill. In
the past God overlooked such ignorance, but now he

commands all people everywhere to repent. For he
has set a day when he will judge the world with justice by the man he has appointed. He has given proof
of this to all men by raising him from the dead.

—Acts 17:24–31

Defining a Worldview

By the time each of us becomes cognizant of the fact that
we have thinking processes, we have already formed certain
assumptions by which those processes operate. These presuppositions are "caught" rather than formally taught, in
most cases. Our experiences and observations, as well as input
from others, cause us to assume certain things about the
world and about the way things in general work.

Because these things seem self-evident to us (in the words
of my father-in-law, "Any durn fool can see it"), we don't
give much thought to them until they are challenged by
someone with different presuppositions, or until someone
else draws deliberate attention to them.

The combination of these presuppositions makes up a person's worldview. One friend of mine describes worldview as
a grid that is located just in front of our eyeballs, through
which all the information we see is sifted. Another analogy I
have heard is of file folders in which we sort facts and impres-
sions for later use. Once the "labels" are in place, of course,
it's difficult to go back and reorganize that thought system.

It almost goes without saying that people do not always
sort information according to assumptions that are biblically
based. In fact, the Bible even contains several anecdotes that
illustrate this.

One such story is found in Acts chapter 14. Paul and Barnabas were in the Asian town of Lystra, where they healed a
man who had been lame since birth. A crowd of people soon
gathered and assessed the situation according to their Greek

worldview. They assumed that any supernatural acts must have their source in the gods that they knew. When presented with an undeniable healing of a man before their very eyes, they combined this present experience with their presuppositions and came to the conclusion that Paul and Barnabas must be gods. They even went so far as to identify them as Zeus and Hermes.

When Paul and Barnabas heard of this, two things of note happened. First, they were distraught at this misunderstanding and tried to convince the people that another explanation for what had happened existed. Second, the reaction of the people when their worldview was challenged was also notable. After being swayed by Jews from Antioch, they turned on Paul, stoned him, and left him for dead.

Now, I bring up this story to illustrate two points. First, I believe the Bible is such a marvelous instrument that there is no error of the human mind it does not anticipate and in some way respond to. Second, I also love this story of Paul and Barnabas because it so aptly confirms my contention that having one's worldview questioned or challenged is not usually a comfortable experience. In fact, it can be disorienting and frightening.

The Worldview Shift

Leaving a cult necessitates a worldview shift, because someone who has been deeply involved in a cult has had his or her thinking prescribed by the worldview of that organization. A person cannot just try to juggle opposing worldviews. James says that a double-minded man is unstable in all he does and should not dare to think that God can bless him in such a condition (James 1:7–8.) Nor can a person just refuse to decide and go along with the pluralistic views our society seems to demand (You're simply not tolerant, they say, if you don't accept all creeds as having equal validity), because lukewarmness is something God spews out of his mouth in disgust (Rev. 3:16).

Those who have grown up in traditional Christianity tend to assume when someone makes a worldview shift and goes from cultic thinking to biblical truth that it is a joyful experience. It is not always so. Consider the fact that much of a Mormon's thinking—especially that which has to do with his dreams and aspirations according to which his actions conform—revolves around his plan to become a god and live with his family forever. Now, while the Christian thinks that such dreams are groundless to begin with, the ex-Mormon who realizes with a crash that he's spent all that emotional energy on a dream that will never be realized feels *robbed*. It's like scrimping and saving to pay insurance premiums and finding out late in life that the agent has been pocketing the money, taking his own family on expensive vacations, and has known all the while that the company to which you thought you were paying premiums went bankrupt and out of business fifty years ago.

With this in mind, I believe one of the first elements that must be accepted by Christians dealing with ex-Mormons is the dynamic of loss. When people feel that they have been deprived of something that was important to them, they often react in ways that seem to be inexplicable. Their actions and reactions may not be commensurate to a situation at hand and may reflect anger, disappointment, even resentment that can surface later.

I believe that being able to understand the worldview of someone is an important step in teaching that person. It requires "seeing where he's coming from." However, people have been successfully extracted from cults and firmly rooted in biblical truth by teachers who never heard of worldview nor even thought about its existence. Assessing worldview, then, is a tool, not an end in itself. But it is a very valuable tool.

Five Elements Comprising a Worldview

James W. Sire, in his book *The Universe Next Door*, says that a well-rounded worldview answers the following questions:

> What is prime or basic reality—the really real?
> Who is man?
> What happens to man at death?
> What is the basis for morality?
> What is the meaning of human history?

Now, whether or not we have ever sat down and thought consciously about these things, almost all of us have certain preconceptions concerning each. Again, what we think in each of these areas seems so logical and natural that it is hard for us sometimes to understand how someone else could possibly come to conclusions other than those we have come to.

The biblical worldview has a distinctive profile. According to Sire, the Bible answers those five questions like this:

1. *What is the most real thing in existence?* In brief, Sire says that the Bible shows God to be the being basic to existence. He describes the God of the Bible as being the following:

> Infinite (He alone is self-existent, the source of all other reality and beyond any sort of quantification.)
> Personal (More than just a force, he has personality and self-awareness and the ability to act alone.)
> Triune (Three personalities, all of whom can correctly be said to be God, exist coequally and coeternally.)
> Transcendent (God is beyond us and our world, not just like us.)
> Immanent (As spirit, God is able to be in all and sustain all.)

Omniscient (The source of all wisdom and intelligence, he is aware of everything.)

Sovereign (God is interested in and in authority over everything.)

Good (Not only is God the source of all goodness but he actually embodies it. He is the standard against which everything else is assessed.)

Creator of the universe (He created it out of nothing—a cosmos planned to be orderly without being determined.)

God communicates with man through both general and specific revelation.

2. *Who is man?* Sire says the Bible teaches that humanity is created in God's image. This means that humans are like God and reflect some of the qualities of God by possessing the following:

Personality (People are self-conscious and self-determining.)

Self-transcendence (People have ability to control their actions and reactions, not just respond to their surroundings.)

Intelligence (ability to know and to reason)

Morality (ability to distinguish good from evil)

Gregariousness (need for social contact)

Creativity (imagination)

In addition, the Bible teaches that people, though created good, fell and "defaced" their reflection of God. They are capable of being redeemed by the atonement of Christ and ultimately glorified after death in full reconciliation with God.

3. *What happens to humans at death?* Sire states, "For man death is either the gate to life with God and His people, or the gate to eternal separation from the only thing that will ultimately fulfill man's aspirations."

4. *What is the basis for morality?* Sire says that the Bible bases all ethics on the personality of God. They are transmitted through his revealed Word. As such, they cannot depend upon either humanity's or culture's judgment alone.

5. *What is the meaning of human history?* Sire identifies the biblical view of history as linear in that events are meaningful, sequential (not cyclical), and lead to the ultimate fulfillment of God's stated purposes. (There is some disagreement among Bible scholars with Sire's linear view of history.)

Dealing with Opposing Worldviews

Now, as you read through these five "slots" of worldview, if you are a Christian you probably found nothing there that challenged your thinking. Perhaps some of the terminology was a little unfamiliar, but the concepts were familiar. But if you have spent much time talking to someone from another culture, you will find that the vast majority of people in this world operate on different suppositions. Hindus, for instance, have a full range of gods from the benign to the bloodthirsty. Your New Age neighbor sees man as the receptacle and the embodiment of God. The multiple millions of Buddhists on this planet believe death is just the doorway to rebirth into another body and lifetime. If statistics accurately reflect American ethics, what is right is what feels right. And the view held by most primitive cultures as well as New Age believers is that history is either cyclical or meaningless.

As I mentioned before, our suppositions in these five areas cause us to interpret things differently. One person can see an event and draw certain conclusions, while another observer of the same event "sees" something else. An example of this is demonstrated in Acts 28. When Paul and his companions were shipwrecked after a terrible storm at sea, they found themselves on the island of Malta. The natives who lived there showed them "unusual kindness" and obviously had a worldview that included a concept of some sort of divine vindication. When a poisonous snake fastened itself onto Paul's hand, they reasoned that he must be a murderer ("Though he escaped from the sea, Justice has not allowed him to live"). When Paul was unharmed by the snake, they changed their minds, deciding that he must be a god.

Now, everyone in the shipwrecked party saw the same snake, but only the natives came to those conclusions. That was because they were struggling to fit what they saw into their preconceptions, trying to process the data of their observations and make it fit into their worldview. This is the way all people respond to new information. They try to make it fit into their presumptions. Only a major questioning of those presumptions can lead to a worldview shift.

I mentioned before that the Bible's genius is revealed in the way it seems to anticipate many concerns, even before we articulate them. In the passage that opened this chapter, I quoted from Paul's famous sermon on Mars Hill in Acts 17. Look at how Paul assessed the worldview of his listeners and then answered questions from the five categories.

1. *What is the most real thing in existence?* Paul directed their attention to the many altars there, then centered on that of the unknown God, who has the following characteristics: He made the world; he is Lord of heaven and earth; he is not confined by physical walls; he is the source of all things including life itself; he is interested in humankind and seeks contact with people; he is nearby; he is not made in the image of man.

2. *Who is man?* Humanity had its beginning in one created man. Its source of life and being is God, it is the "offspring" of God, it cannot formulate God but is instead defined by him.

3. *What happens to humans at death?* God will judge the world at a preset date. Resurrection is a historical reality.

4. *What is the basis for morality?* God commands all people everywhere to repent. Justice will be administered through

the person of Jesus Christ, whose authority is proved by his resurrection.

5. *What is the meaning of human history?* All humanity is descended from one God-created man; God determined the times and places where people would live; ignorance of God has in the past been overlooked, but now repentance is required; a certain date has been set for the judgment of humanity; the historic event of Jesus' resurrection is pivotal.

Isn't it interesting how Paul, in his one shot at this crowd, responded to all of these elements that make up worldview? Now, I admit that he never intended this to be a complete treatise on Christianity. But I am grateful for this scriptural example of a way to deal with a very different worldview.

It is also interesting to see the results that Paul's challenge of the prevailing worldview produced. Acts 17 goes on to show us that there were three reactions: Some sneered; some expressed interest and wanted to hear more; and some, only a few, "became followers of Paul and believed" (which, I think, indicates that they made a decision to try to adopt his worldview and abandon their own, at least concerning the matters Paul spoke about).

Similarly, the person who decides to leave Mormonism makes a decision to abandon a worldview. However, adopting the worldview of the Bible is far from automatic. Many, many people leave Mormonism and decide that there is no God, that people are on their own and must make up their own morality, that life after death is "iffy," and that the individual's life span is, in effect, the history of his world. In other words, many people leave Mormonism and, somewhat by default, become humanists.

If the person you are teaching has joined a church for what seems to you to be purely social reasons, perhaps you should consider the possibility that although he has left Mormonism, he may still be weighing his options as far as Christianity is concerned. If you perceive that to be true, you might recommend that your friend read *Mere Christianity* by C. S.

Lewis, or John R. W. Stott's *Basic Christianity*, both of which are aimed at people who do not assume that Christianity is the only way.

The Mormon Worldview

Let's take a look at the way Mormons are taught to process information according to the five elements of a worldview and compare them to Sire's assessment of Christianity in the ways that it answers the five basic questions. It is beyond the scope of this book to document all the elements I will deal with here; however, if you wish to look at Mormon doctrine and practice from its own sources, I would recommend the following books:

> *A Marvelous Work and a Wonder* by LeGrand Richards
> *One Lord, One Faith!* by Mark E. Petersen
> *Mormon Doctrine* by Bruce R. McConkie

All of these books are by Mormons, primarily for Mormons and prospective converts to the Mormon Church. They deal with Mormon doctrine in easy-to-read sections and are available in your local LDS bookstore (store name available by calling a local LDS ward). You will see that they are very persuasive and operate out of the following assumptions: The Bible is incomplete and in some cases misleading; the true church was taken off the earth at the death of the last apostle; and priesthood "authority" is necessary for church legitimacy.

I would also recommend the following three books, which document Mormon doctrine from Mormon sources but are written by ex-Mormons:

> *Mormonism: Shadow or Reality?* by Jerald and Sandra Tanner, Modern Microfilm, 1982. Available through

Lighthouse Ministry, P.O. Box 1844, Salt Lake City, UT 84110. Comprehensive and thorough.

Where Does It Say That? by Bob Witte, Gospel Truths Ministry, Grand Rapids, Michigan. Available from them or from Concerned Christians and Former Mormons, 14106 Whittier Blvd., Whitter, CA 90605. Primarily photo-reprints of LDS documents that show inconsistencies.

The Mormon Mirage by Latayne Scott (Zondervan, 1979). Heavily footnoted for further study.

Please avail yourself of one or more of these books if you wish to document any aspect of the following five areas of Mormon worldview.

These views are abbreviated below so as to give you a general impression of the vast differences that exist between what Mormonism teaches and what the Bible alone teaches. I have tried to define Mormonism *as the average Mormon today would understand it*, not as practiced in the distant past nor only as scholars would define it. If you are going to try to combat the Mormon worldview as held by the "Mormon on the street," you need as little "clutter" as possible.

1. *LDS: What is the most real thing in existence?* A Mormon would undoubtedly answer this question by saying that God is the most real thing in existence. Let's compare Sire's aspects of God to what Mormons believe. First of all, when a Mormon uses the term *God*, he is referring only to the Father. Jesus Christ and the Holy Ghost are two completely separate beings. While the origins of the Holy Ghost—the only one of the LDS triad without a corporeal body—are obscure, Mormon doctrine teaches that Jesus is literally God's son, having been born spiritually in the preexistence and then born physically through the Father's contact with the young girl Mary on earth.

While Christians believe God is infinite, Mormon doctrine suggests a time when God himself was created by another

god above him. Thus, the God of the Bible is not the ultimate reality at all.

When Mormons agree with Christians that God is personal they mean it much more literally than Christians. They
believe that God was once a man who lived on an earth somewhere and as a result of his good life was rewarded with godhood by *his* god. Thus Mormons believe that he can truly
identify with their life struggles. However, he is not completely sovereign for two reasons. First, he is subject to his
own father-god, and second, Mormon doctrine teaches that
even he must obey and work within specific natural laws (gravity, for instance). Miracles, therefore, are to the Mormon
mind the operation by God of other physical laws that supersede laws with which we are familiar but which must,
nonetheless, be obeyed by God.

Mormon doctrine explicitly denies the Trinity doctrine to
the point of public ridicule of it and is emphatic in its asser-
tions that the three elements of the Trinity are separate in
every way except in purpose. Jesus Christ, specifically, was
brought into being by God the Father and thus cannot in
any way be said to be coeternal with God. As one who also
had to come to an earth to gain a body and thus achieve godhood, Jesus is always a sort of "junior partner" to his father.

The Mormon god cannot be said to be transcendent nor
immanent, for he, like us, is said to have a physical body of
flesh and bones. When Mormons speak of man being made
in God's image, they are talking of the physical similarity of
appearance of the bodies. The Mormon god emphatically is
not just spirit, cannot indwell as Christians understand the
word. He dwells on a planet, Mormons teach, somewhere
near a star they call Kolob.

As himself just one in a long line of gods whose origin is
hidden, the Mormon god is not the source of all wisdom and
intelligence. However, before he became a god he, like all
other gods and humans, existed first as "pure intelligence"

before being "organized" and given a spirit body by his god-parents.

The Mormon god is portrayed as being keenly interested in his children here on earth but hampered somewhat by the fact that he can only be in one place at one time. The Holy Ghost of Mormonism provides communication between this being and people, for the Holy Ghost, unlike the other two members of the Godhead, does not have a physical body and can operate more widely. However, he cannot indwell a person, either, in the way Christians believe is possible, because each believer already has a resident spirit (his own) filling his body. Mormon doctrine also differentiates between the Spirit of Christ (available to anyone) and the Holy Ghost (only given to Mormons at their confirmation after baptism).

The sovereignty of the Mormon god is delegated largely to his church, specifically its priesthood leaders, who are believed to represent him on earth. Because of this, for many Mormons the church itself is the most real thing in existence, for, in the absence of a perceived personal relationship with the Mormon god, it dominates their lives and their thinking.

While the Mormon god is portrayed as being supremely good, he cannot be said to be perfectly so, because he, like all other rational creatures, is involved in a process known as eternal progression, in which the passage of time finds him becoming more good. Nor can he, as one of a line of gods, be said to be the source of good except as it is known and conveyed to his creatures here on this earth and the many other earths he created and peopled.

The status of Mormonism's father-god as creator of the world is somewhat ambiguous, for doctrine teaches that, though he through the spirit-birth process with his wives created the spirits of all humans before they were born onto this earth, he himself was not personally involved in the making of the earth (a job assigned to his firstborn spirit child, Jesus, following a battle with his second spirit child, Lucifer, who was thereafter banished from heaven and punished by never being able to have a body).

The universe was not, Mormons teach, created out of nothing but was the result of the "organization" of pre-existing elements, done according to physical laws under which this god operated.

Mormon doctrine teaches that its god much more openly communicates with mankind than the God of the Bible, whom they see as having been completely mute for the past two thousand years. In contrast, the LDS god speaks to the head of the Mormon Church on a regular basis on matters of contemporary importance, as well as through other leaders to guide them and those under their influence.

2. *LDS: Who is man?* Perhaps the most succinct way of dealing with this question is to quote Mormon prophet Lorenzo Snow, who said, "As man is, God once was; as God is, man may become." Other Mormon writers have referred to man as "god in embryo." He possesses most of the same qualities as the Mormon god; he is just not as far along in the process of eternal progression. Man is eternal in the same way the Mormon god is eternal, having existed first as an intelligence, then as a spirit, then in earth life, and later (potentially) as a god.

Mormons do not believe in the fall of Adam in the same way Christians do. Mormon writer Sterling W. Sill put it this way: "Adam fell, but he fell upward." The choice to disobey God in the Garden of Eden is seen by Mormons as a necessary step in allowing Adam and Eve to be able to reproduce. Their actions were sin only in the sense that they transgressed a commandment, but, Mormons believe, they did it to bring about a greater good—the peopling of the earth. Thus the LDS god from the very beginning put humans into a dilemma of opposing commandments, neither of which they could obey while obeying the other.

Therefore, according to LDS doctrine, humanity has no original sin for which any atonement is necessary. Instead, the ability to sin necessitates the provision of water baptism at the age of eight (the age of accountability). Adults who come to Mormonism have prior sins washed away in baptism but are capable of committing certain sins (adultery, murder) that even Jesus cannot atone for and for which they themselves must pay. However, LDS doctrine sees humans overall as inherently noble and capable of assuming the responsibilities of godhood if they are properly trained.

Along the same lines, Mormons believe that marriage and the family unit are eternal when sealed in a Mormon temple. One of the great motivations for leading a good life as a Mormon is the hope of being able to be with one's loved ones throughout eternity.

3. *LDS: What happens to humans at death?* The Mormon view of the afterlife is detailed. Mormons believe that at the point of death, a person's spirit (a refined substance of specific size and recognizability) continues to live on earth with the spirits of all others who have died. A preliminary judgment at the point of each individual's death divides people who have lived good lives from those who have lived evil lives, regardless of religion (paradise and spirit prison). Mormons in paradise are allowed to interact with other good spirits as well as those of evil people in prison by teaching them the Mormon gospel, which may be accepted in this state as if in earth life. Meanwhile, living people perform proxy baptism, marriages, and sealings for such souls who need it.

After a series of resurrections on earth, at a final judgment, people are consigned to the celestial kingdom (faithful Mormons who have been married in the temple, served by other faithful Mormons who were not), the terrestrial kingdom (lukewarm Mormons as well as others—honorable people who accepted proxy baptism after being taught Mormonism in the spirit world), and the telestial kingdom (home of wicked people who must atone for their own sins through the millennium), or to hell (a place populated by a very few apostates from Mormonism whose bodies are not resurrected). Different Mormon apologists disagree about whether or not one can progress upward from one kingdom to another.

4. *LDS: What is the basis for morality?* As was seen above in the discussion of the Mormon view of original sin, it is difficult for Mormons to agree about what sin actually is. But I think most Mormons would agree that, while their scriptures are important, the final arbiter of what is right and wrong is the church's leadership at the time. The Mormon god can and does often change his mind about what is appropriate (example: the practice of polygamy), but Mormons see it as his way of protecting his people and staying abreast of changing conditions in the world.

5. *LDS: What is the meaning of human history?* Mormons are uniquely interested in three aspects of history. First, they chart history as having unseeable origins in the gods above the god of this world. Second, they believe that for about eighteen hundred years the true gospel did not exist on the earth, necessitating a restoration brought about through the agency of Joseph Smith. This man, they say, did more for the salvation of humankind than anyone else except Jesus. Third, Mormonism is uniquely an American religion, not only because of its origin but because it teaches that this nation's Constitution and other documents were formulated under the direction of the Holy Ghost and that almost all of its presidents have become Mormons in the spirit world. The final triumph and vindication of the Mormon religion in the near future is devoutly looked for by most Mormons, who believe that Brigham Young prophesied that Mormon priesthood will save the United States Constitution at a future time when it will "hang by a thread." In addition, they see the exponential growth of their church worldwide as undeniable proof of its validity.

Once you digest these elements of worldview that Mormons hold, you will see why it is at first difficult for them to admit that man is a fallen creature, or that God cannot be seen or touched, or that death will end their marriage relationships.

These points of basic belief are, as I mentioned before, the domain of loss and mourning. It is my plea to those teaching ex-Mormons that they accompany them with sympathy and allow them, like Jephtha's daughter, a time to mourn for those things they dreamed of which will never be.

4

The Four Epistemologies: How We Know What We Know

My purpose is

    A. That they may be encouraged in heart

    B. [That they may be] united in love

        1. So that they may have the full riches of complete understanding

        2. In order that they may know the mystery of God

            a. Namely, Christ

            b. In whom are hidden all the treasures of wisdom and knowledge.

I tell you this so that no one may deceive you by fine-sounding arguments.

See to it that no one takes you captive through hollow and deceptive philosophy

    A. Which depends on human tradition

    B. [Which depends on] the basic principles of this world

    C. Rather than on Christ.

—Colossians 2:2–4, 8 (arranged by author)

The Four Secular Epistemologies

For a long time now, the world has been telling us Christians that there are only four divisions to epistemology, or ways to know something.

Let's consider the case of a man who walks out onto his back porch to enjoy a sunset. He can feel the heat of the sun's rays on his face, and he recognizes that the sun is the source of that heat. He observes the fact that the sun seems to be nearing the horizon, but he was taught in school that in actuality the earth is turning on its axis. He combines his observation of the low-hanging clouds he sees with the weather report he has just heard, which predicted hail, and he moves his patio tomato plant under the eave. Finally, he sits down in his chair and basks in the beauty of what he sees.

This fictional vignette illustrates the four ways of knowing, or epistemologies, that the world says are the media through which we learn: empiricism, authority, reason, and intuition.

Empiricism, Authority, Reason, and Intuition Defined

The first epistemology through which we all learn is empiricism, or direct observation. It is the way our sunset observer feels the heat on his face and knows that it comes from the sun.

Long before we learn to communicate with words, we learn many things from our own experience. A baby learns that crying can bring Mom to meet the needs of hunger, thirst, or a clean diaper. One experience with touching a hot oven teaches even a small child not to repeat the action. Later, we draw conclusions from other things we personally see, hear, taste, smell, and feel. The process we refer to as the scientific method is based on empiricism.

A second epistemology is authority, or historical learning.

As opposed to direct experience, this way of knowing takes place when someone passes along the experiences of others. It is the way the man watching the sunset knows that the sun is not actually moving as it seems.

The mechanisms of the epistemology of authority come into play early in our lives. Most children, for instance, do not personally experience being hit by a car, because their parents have impressed on them the importance of taking their word for the fact that such an action would be disastrous. At the other end of life, scholars study other cultures and peoples to try to assess what they did that ultimately benefited or hurt them. By studying others' mistakes, we do not have to empirically experience their effects ourselves.

Reason, the third way of knowing, occurs when we use information along with the mechanism of logic to come to conclusions that we have not necessarily experienced directly nor been told of by other persons. By the comparison of two or more ideas, a "new" discovery is made. The man watching the sunset, for instance, used two facts to come to the conclusion that he should move his tomato plant out of the way of the hailstones he has concluded might fall on the plant.

The fourth epistemology is intuition. Both observing and defining this way of knowing is extremely slippery. Intuition involves the very personal concepts of such things as feeling, appreciation, creativity, and other qualities we put under the umbrella term *subjectivity*. Intuition does not yield itself to analysis by empiricism, authority, or reason. It is the way the man watching the sunset can "know" that what he sees is beautiful.

The Four Epistemologies in Scripture

Of course, we can find evidence in Scripture for each of these epistemologies. Empiricism, or direct observation, is a way through which God has allowed himself to be known throughout history to all peoples, as we can read in Romans:

For since the creation of the world God's invisible qualities—
his eternal power and divine nature—have been clearly seen,
being understood from what has been made, so that men are
without excuse.

Romans 1:20

Reason is certainly a method of "coming to know" that is
used in the Bible. The apostle Paul used it extensively. One
of the most memorable examples of his use of logic is seen
in 1 Corinthians chapter 15. Here Paul shows that there must
be a coming resurrection of the dead. Those who teach that
there is no resurrection, he reasons, must necessarily along
with that deny the resurrection of Jesus, without which there
is no basis for the Christian faith as a whole.

Intuition, the way of knowing that has a purely internal
source within the learner, is also dealt with in the Bible,
although usually not kindly. While the subjective sense is used
sometimes positively (for instance, the Word is said to be
"sweeter than honey"), the heart, or subjective source, is,
according to Jeremiah 17:9, "deceitful above all things." We
love all the Scripture passages that tell us to hide the Word
in our hearts and have pure hearts, but a quick scan of the
Book of Proverbs also finds descriptions of hearts that lust,
spurn correction, devise wickedness, and are perverse, proud,
and full of rage against God. The Book of Judges also shows
what happens when a people operate only on what "seems
right" to each individual: a chaotic society resulting from
each man doing "as he saw fit" (Judges 17:6; 21:25).

The Bible leans very heavily on the epistemology of authority. The King James Version of Galatians 3:24 refers to the
law as a schoolmaster, or teacher. The entire Bible, in fact,
presents itself as a historical record of events and thoughts of
real people. Some of its writers were meticulous in docu-
menting its historicity (look at how Luke pinned down the
dates of John the Baptist's ministry in Luke 3:1–2), while
others, like the apostle John, made sure that the reader would
understand the source of the veracity of their words:

That which was from the beginning, which we have heard, which we have seen with our eyes, which we have looked at and our hands have touched—this we proclaim concerning the Word of life.

1 John 1:1

An appeal to authority through history is certainly a valid way of teaching someone about Christ. After all, we know what we know about the historical Jesus through the documents of the New Testament. However, teaching someone only through this method of coming to know leads to legalism—a cut-and-dried way of looking at issues that can suppress other epistemologies. Reason, or dependence on pure logic, likewise, if used exclusively can lead to arrogance. Empiricism, or observation, if used exclusively can make a naturalist out of any learner who is trained to make judgments only on the basis of his or her own experience and observations.

Most dangerous of all to use alone is intuition; yet it is the way that most people make many important decisions. One of the best examples of this is the way that many people approach voting for political candidates. Most people do not have personal acquaintance with a candidate or his actions (cannot use empiricism), do not examine his stand on a full range of past issues (no appeal to authority or historical epistemology), feel they have insufficient information to reason or predict future actions on the basis of past ones (do not operate on reason or logic). But most people walk into the voting booth and pull the lever next to the name of the person who makes them *feel* a certain way (intuition).

The Four Epistemologies as Used by Mormons

Now what has all this to do with teaching a new, ex-Mormon Christian?

First, it is important for teacher and student to evaluate the ways in which these four traditionally defined epistemologies are used in Mormonism.

Empiricism, or personal experience, holds a uniquely sovereign role in the practice of Mormonism. Remember the letter I quoted at length in chapter 1 from the young woman Diane who observed that her child was healed from meningitis following a priesthood blessing by a Mormon bishop. She put aside all her doubts about the veracity of Mormon doctrine because of that one experience.

An appeal to personal experience is the cornerstone on which Mormonism is built. A desire to know, once and for all, which church is right—to be answered directly from God—is what makes the Joseph Smith story of kneeling in a grove praying for guidance so potent an appeal in our confused and pluralistic world. It is why so many prospective converts to Mormonism will wade through reading the *Book of Mormon*; they can have hope of the "burning in the bosom" that this book claims will confirm its own truthfulness.

Authority, or an appeal to history, is also a very important Mormon tenet. (But be careful. *Authority* is a supercharged word to Mormons. To them, it means the God-given right to exercise ecclesiastical functions such as performing baptisms and ordaining people to priesthood positions. This authorization is not the epistemology of authority under discussion here.) To Mormons, the way of knowing that we have previously defined and refer to as authority encompasses such powerful elements as heritage as well as their (narrowly defined) history.

The issue of heritage is not to be underestimated. I know of no other major American religious group (with the exception of Orthodox Judaism and possibly Amish Christianity) in which heritage and culture play such an important role in the thinking of the individual member. Anyone who has lived in Utah, or even visited there for any length of time, needs no explanation of the pervasive nature of Mormonism there. It is not just a religion, it is a culture. As such, it affects the thinking of its people in a way that must be appreciated and dealt with.

The issue of history is also significant. While the Mormon Church itself owns "original manuscripts"—papers and journals from founders of their religion—that are only, say, a hundred years old, members-at-large are often restricted in their access to such things. About ten years ago, Mormon apostle Boyd K. Packer urged Mormon historians to only write "faithful history," which he defined as accounts that bolster belief and avoid awkward or embarrassing details that would weaken faith. (Using those guidelines, a "faithful history" Bible, for example, might omit Abraham's lies about Sarah, David's adultery, and Peter's denials of Christ.)

The end result of such thinking is that the Mormon's authority epistemology is often limited by "sanitized" versions of his own church's history.

Reason is important to Mormons. I believe that, of all the accusations that can be made against present-day Mormon doctrine as it is practiced and understood by most Mormons, one cannot say that it is illogical. If a person accepts the premises that (1) God appeared to Joseph Smith and has continued to lead the subsequent leaders of the Mormon Church to produce the scriptures and tenets it has, and (2) this deity (as defined by Mormon doctrine as a former human in continuing progress) can "refine" or even reverse any teachings, then to that person Mormonism (within its own parameters) is quite orderly.

On the other hand, a lot of the reasoning "tools" we use in the study of Christian doctrine—word studies of the original languages, examination of ancient documents—are absent in textual criticism of Mormon scriptures. Why? The documents of the *Book of Mormon*, for instance, exist only in English. So a lot of the "reasoning" that we Christians do in textual criticism is a process that is foreign (no humor intended) to the average Mormon.

Now, it is absolutely true that Christians can be legitimately strengthened in *their* faith by personal experience, by identification with Christian history and heritage, by the ability to show logical reasons for their hope, and by subjective feelings of satisfaction (called joy, peace, or blessedness). How, then, is the Christian use of these four epistemologies any different from that of the Mormon?

There is a significant way in which they differ. It is based on the fact that Christian faith is only unmistakably validated through Jesus Christ as he is revealed through the Word. The Book of Romans puts it this way: "Faith comes from hearing the message, and the message is heard through the word of Christ" (10:17). Any Christian's faith that is based more on personal experience or logic or feelings than on the primary authority of the personality and redemption of Jesus as pictured throughout the Bible is a precarious faith.

Epistemology in a Mormon "Testimony"

The faith of the typical Mormon is similarly precarious. I sat through hundreds of "fast-and-testimony" meetings held on the first Sunday of each month when I was a Mormon. I heard literally thousands of testimonies, which, almost without exception, said something to this effect: "I know that the Mormon Church is the true church, and that Joseph Smith was a prophet, and that there is a prophet at the head of the church today." Such a testimony would usually go on to include details of how the individual speaking had been helped by living Mormon doctrine and by feelings of love for family members and other fellow members.

Let's examine the individual elements of such a testimony. Only one element can be said to be epistemologically perceived by empiricism: the fact that there is someone at the head of the LDS church who is called by the title of prophet. One can personally experience the prophet's existence by watching him on television or by seeing him in April and October at General Conference in Salt Lake City. According to the Mormon definition of the word, he is a prophet because that is one of the titles—seer and revelator are others—that Mormons use to describe the president of their church.

However, the assessment that such a man is a prophet according to the biblical definition can hardly be based on reason, for Deuteronomy 18:20–22 says that a true prophet cannot speak presumptuously in the name of god or gods other than the God of the Bible or by falsely predicting an event that does not come to pass.

When a Mormon says that he knows that the Mormon Church is the true church, he is not talking about the result of an empirical survey in which it was compared with all other churches, nor an evaluation of what truth means. He is speaking of knowledge that is the result of intuition, authority, and reason (in that order). When questioned closely, the main proof of his claim to know that the Mormon Church is true will, in most cases, be based on the fact that (1) he feels it in his heart (often as the result of a "burning in the bosom," a phenomenon to be discussed in detail later); (2) because he has been so taught by people whose judgment and discernment he trusts; (3) he will believe that he has been tangibly blessed for his decision to be—or become—a Mormon; and (4) (least often true in the case of lifelong Mormons who have not served missions) because he has used reason and logic to determine the nature of the church.

The person who served as a missionary and/or was converted to the Mormon Church through the missionary "discussions" will believe that he or she made (or reaffirmed) the decision to embrace Mormonism through logic. This is a valid assessment, because the highly structured lessons use many of the mechanisms of logic. For instance, an "investigator" will be asked by a missionary, "Since God promised in the Book of Amos that he would not do anything without revealing it to a prophet, and we deal with many issues that the Bible does not address, doesn't that prove that we need a prophet today who can help us with issues that the Bible did not foresee?" As you can probably see, this contains misleading premises that lead—quite logically—to a faulty conclusion.

Pinning Down an Epistemology

Here is the point: Everyone in the world—Christian or pagan, Mormon or non-Mormon—believes that he or she knows certain things. It is very important to be prepared to ask questions of someone to ascertain *how* that person came to the conclusions that would allow him or her to say, "I know this."

When my children were small, someone gave me a very valuable tip. I was told that when my children brought their art work to me, I should not ask, "What is it?" Instead, I should start conversation by saying something like, "Thank you for bringing this to show me! Tell me all about it." A similar technique works well in conversation, too. If you can first affirm the worth of the person with whom you are talking ("Boy, I'm sure glad you can explain things so I can understand where you are coming from"), and then ask him or her to tell you about a concept (such as the Godhead) and the basis on which he or she came to those conclusions, you will save a lot of time and probably spare some pretty tender feelings.

Dealing with the Ex-Mormon's Epistemologies (Empiricism, Authority, Reason, and Intuition)

Here is an example of how this works. If you assume that the ex-Mormon with whom you are studying has based her concept of the role of church leaders upon a detailed study of what the *Doctrine and Covenants* says about the matter, and you try to discuss the difference between her concept of leadership and the Bible's, then you might find a great gulf of communication emerging. What most Mormons know about church leadership is not from doctrinal teachings (the epistemology of authority) but from their own observations of how things worked when they were in a Mormon ward (the epistemology of empiricism). The ex-Mormon might respond to your barrage of information from the *Doctrine and Covenants* by saying something like, "Well, that might be what it says there, but in my experience, it was like this. . . ."

This is where my suggestion in chapter 2, that you keep a notebook and pen handy, comes into play. At this point in the conversation, you might say, "Hey, let's write this down. You said that you saw that missionaries and bishops and other church leaders were willing to give their services to the church without pay, and that was something you felt pretty good about." On further questioning, you will find that from this your ex-Mormon friend will have concluded that paying church workers is actually wrong. She may, from her time in Mormonism, have been given the impression that anyone who takes money for church work is motivated by greed or worse. (Up until just recently a certain section of the temple ceremony depicted a Christian preacher taking money from the devil to preach.) From all this she may have residual, even unconscious, questions about *your* motivations if you are on a church payroll.

Much of what an ex-Mormon knows about doctrine comes through the epistemology of authority—what she has read, heard, or otherwise been taught. Much of this is through weekly classes. What she knows about the Bible in particular is through being told what it says instead of through her own intensive, comprehensive reading of the Bible itself.

There are several reasons for this. First of all, Mormons have four "standard works" of "scripture": the *Book of Mormon*, the *Doctrine and Covenants, The Pearl of Great Price*, as well as the Bible. Since Mormon doctrine teaches that the Bible has been corrupted in the translation process over the last two thousand years, they believe it is by far the least reliable of the four. The sheer bulk of pages contained in four books of scriptures necessitates in the minds of most Mormons a prioritizing. When I was a Mormon, I never was required, nor did I ever take it upon myself, to read the Bible in its entirety. But I thought it was a good backup to the other, more reliable books. With that in mind, I memorized the location of key Scripture passages that I believed supported Mormonism (John 10:16; Ezek. 37:15–20; Isa. 29:4, and others) and could find them with ease. But I spent my quality study time in the other books.

The epistemology of reason is especially noteworthy. As mentioned before, Mormon doctrine follows logically if one accepts the faulty premises on which it is based. The church itself takes great pride in the fact that new or emerging doctrines "dovetail," as they put it, with its teachings of the past. It is true. You could take, say, a recently published class textbook of the history and doctrines of the LDS church and see that everything *in it* is unified. On that basis, a contemporary Mormon who uses such things (as I did) as primary sources of information about the church, its past, and its doctrines, would certainly say that it is harmonious and therefore logical.

Again, it is impossible to overestimate the subjective element's power in the life of an ex-Mormon. Many people leave the Mormon Church at the cost of family (and therefore heritage) and friends, and sometimes even jobs, money, health, and physical safety. At the very least, they lose their god.

The elements of peace of mind, comfort, security, assurance of one's own ability to make good decisions—all of these are precarious to an ex-Mormon. It is especially important to be very sensitive and loving when asking questions about intuitively perceived knowledge that an ex-Mormon may hold, because the identification of something as such may seem to be a judgment on his or her ability to make wise assessments in spiritual matters. If he or she has been standing up in fast-and-testimony meetings for the last twenty years and telling fellow Mormons that "I *know* the Mormon Church is the true church," the discovery that this knowledge was based mainly on subjective feelings will not be of much comfort to the ex-Mormon. Here, more than in empiricism, authority, or logic, the blame would seem to rest on the *individual* who was deceived rather than on the church that did the deceiving.

Correcting the Conclusions of the False Epistemologies

While one might think that the way to correct a false conclusion would be to work with the type of epistemology that led someone to that conclusion, this simply will not work in most cases when dealing with biblical doctrine. The epistemology of authority—to be specific, the teachings of the Bible itself—is the primary and trustworthy way to deal with cultic error.

Let's look at the above four examples of conclusions a Mormon might have made as a result of the four epistemologies. Through empiricism a Mormon may have formulated his opinion of paid church leadership by what he observed about the fact that his Mormon bishops served without pay. Showing him empirically that Christian preachers can be free from greed and yet serve for pay would be time-consuming and difficult. It would be much more effective to show the ex-Mormon that (1) the Bible repeatedly says that those who labor for the gospel are entitled to be financially remunerated (1 Cor. 9:1–14; 2 Cor. 11:8) and (2) Mormon scripture itself commands that bishops, as well as their counselors, be paid (*Doctrine and Covenants* 42:71–73).

In the case of the epistemology of authority, the best way is to show that the Bible passages taught to Mormons to prove authority actually teach against Mormonism. The Isaiah passage mentioned above is especially effective when read in any version other than the King James Version, as is a simple word study of the word the KJV translates as "familiar."

In dealing with the epistemology of reason, if you can pin-point your ex-Mormon friend's premises on which he made his conclusions, and show whether or not the premises are biblical, then you can effectively show whether or not the conclusions were valid. While you would utilize the mechanisms of logic, your primary appeal would be, of course, to the truth-fulness (as determined by harmony with the Bible) of the premises, and not just to rely on the tools of logic that led to the original wrong conclusion. In addition, an exhibit of the way Mormon doctrine has changed throughout history—as well as the way the LDS church has brazenly lied about those changes to artificially impose consistency on its "faithful history"—can be very eye-opening to a former Mormon.

The final category of epistemology—intuition, or the sub-jective realm—needs special, tender care. Again, however, the first basis for filling the intuitive needs must be the Bible. Confidence and peace in the Christian life must have one pri-mary source—the knowledge of God. All the great fellow-ship and love of a new Christian community will not be enough; most ex-Mormons had those things when they were Mormon. Logical thinking will not suffice. Even subjective satisfaction of having made the right decision at last will not be as sufficient as a knowledge of God.

I do not say that a balance of the four epistemologies is needed. While each of the four ways of knowing is valid, they are not all equally suitable for the transmission of biblical truth from one person to another. Without a knowledge of God through the authority epistemology of the unassailably trustworthy Bible, the ex-Mormon will not be equipped to function as a Christian.

But, as the song says, it that all there is?

5

The Christian's Fifth Epistemology: Faith

> Now faith is being sure of what we hope for and certain of what we do not see.
>
> —Hebrews 11:1

When you read the previous chapter, you probably were able to identify instances in your own life when you have been informed by each of the four epistemologies that the world says comprise the way we learn everything. But you undoubtedly recognize that of the four, the authority epistemology—specifically the Bible—has to be *primary*, because it is the only one of those four whose focus is outside the human mind as a source. Now, any Christian who spends much time in meditating on God's Word and in fervent prayer probably also acknowledges an epistemology available to the Christian that is not empiricism or authority or reason or intuition.

The Bible calls this way of knowing by several terms. Perhaps the one most easily accessible to us is the term *insight*. The apostle Paul gave some teachings to his young disciple

1

Timothy and followed them with the directive, "Reflect on what I am saying, for the Lord will give you insight into all this" (2 Tim. 2:7).

With this Paul identified the two elements that are necessary for this other epistemology. He taught a principle to Timothy (the epistemology of authority, here a divinely inspired source), then told the young man to seek something only the Lord could grant—the gift of insight. Unlike intuition, this is something whose source is not from within the individual but from within God.

The same is seen in Ephesians 3:4, which follows some of Paul's teachings on "the mystery of Christ," which he identified as the wonderful news that both Gentiles and Jews would be heirs together in God's kingdom. Paul's advice to the Ephesians to whom he explained these things was that if they would read what he had written them on this matter, they, too, would be able to understand his insight. Further on he prayed to God to give his readers power to enable them to understand Christ's love and to "know this love which surpasses knowledge" (v. 19).

Now, obviously, this source of information for the Ephesians was not only through direct observation, nor from hearing Paul's words, nor from a logical argument, nor even solely from their own intuition. Paul spoke of a knowing that would be transmitted by other means.

The Other Way of Knowing

Once you start looking in Scripture for this fifth epistemology, it jumps out at you practically from every page of the New Testament. We don't normally think of love as the source of being able to know or understand, but consider what Paul said to the Philippians:

> And this is my prayer: that your love may abound more and more in knowledge and depth of insight, so that you may be

able to discern what is best and may be pure and blameless until the day of Christ.

Philippians 1:9–10

Similarly, Paul told the Colossians he was praying that they would have knowledge of God's will through the same epistemology, "through all spiritual wisdom and understanding" (Col. 1:9). He later went on to tell them that two qualities, encouragement of heart and unity in love, would give them "the riches of complete understanding" (2:2).

We make a mistake when we believe what the world tells us about the four epistemologies being the only ways that knowledge can be transmitted. The gospel *is not just any knowledge,* and its transmission is not restricted to those four epistemologies. Paul made this very clear in 1 Thessalonians when he stated, "Our gospel came to you not simply with words, but also with power, with the Holy Spirit and with deep conviction" (v. 5).

This Scripture text shows that the epistemology of authority—words—was definitely involved. As was discussed in the previous chapter, Bible knowledge is undoubtedly transmitted through the four epistemologies that the world recognizes. Under discussion here is the fifth epistemology, the epistemology available only to Christians, the epistemology of faith.

The Bible speaks of this fifth way of knowing in terms that I believe make clear it is something beyond normal knowing and that it is a unique feature of the new covenant of which Christ is high priest. In Hebrews 8 we read this:

> The time is coming, declares the Lord,
>   when I will make a new covenant
> with the house of Israel
>   and with the house of Judah.
> It will not be like the covenant
>   I made with their forefathers
> when I took them by the hand
>   to lead them out of Egypt,

> because they did not remain faithful to my
> covenant,
> and I turned away from them,
> declares the Lord.
> This is the covenant I will make with the
> house of Israel
> after that time, declares the Lord.
> I will put my laws in their minds
> and write them on their hearts.
> I will be their God,
> and they will be my people.
> No longer will a man teach his neighbor,
> or a man his brother, saying, "Know the Lord,"
> because they will all know me,
> from the least of them to the greatest.
> For I will forgive their wickedness
> and will remember their sins no more.

This new-covenant way of knowing is also described in 1 John 2:27: "The anointing you received from him remains in you, and you do not need anyone to teach you. But as his anointing teaches you about all things and as that anointing is real, not counterfeit—just as it has taught you, remain in him."

Second Corinthians 5:7 juxtaposes faith and sight. Faith, in addition, is something that is received (2 Peter 1:1), and, along with knowledge, is "resting on the hope of eternal life" (Titus 1:2). Neither the Peter nor Titus passage lends much support to the cultic supposition that faith has to be earned, or "worked at." Galatians 3:23, in fact, talks of it as something revealed.

This epistemology is not available to unbelievers, so we should not be surprised that it is not recognized by the world. Paul spoke in 2 Corinthians 4:3–6 of the fact that unbelievers are not able to see in the same way Christians can:

> And even if our gospel is veiled, it is veiled to those who are
> perishing. The god of this age has blinded the minds of unbe-

lievers, so that they cannot see the light of the gospel of the glory of Christ, who is the image of God. For we do not preach ourselves, but Jesus Christ as Lord, and ourselves as your servants for Jesus' sake. For God, who said, "Let light shine out of darkness," made his light shine in our hearts to give us the light of the knowledge of the glory of God in the face of Christ.

Paul also is quite definite in affirming the difference in the way Christians can understand from the way unbelievers cannot. He said in Ephesians 4:17:

So I tell you this, and insist on it in the Lord, that you must no longer live as the Gentiles do, in the futility of their thinking. They are darkened in their understanding and separated from the life of God because of the ignorance that is in them due to the hardening of their hearts. Having lost all sensitivity, they have given themselves over to sensuality so as to indulge in every kind of impurity, with a continual lust for more. You, however, did not come to know Christ that way. Surely you heard of him and were *taught in him* in accordance with the truth that is in Jesus. (italics mine)

Since the world does not recognize this way of knowing or acknowledge its existence, it is no surprise that any evidence of it is passed off merely as intuition. However, to the Christian there is a vast difference between intuition, whose source is human and purely internal, and this insight, whose source is God alone.

This means that this other epistemology, faith, cannot be "mustered up" by autonomous man. Most of the examples I have given from Paul's writings, for instance, are accompanied by his prayer that people be given access to this spiritual insight. This is most obvious in Ephesians 1:17–19:

I keep asking that the God of our Lord Jesus Christ, the glorious Father, may give you the Spirit of wisdom and revelation, so that you may know him better. *I pray also that the eyes of your heart may be enlightened in order that you may know* the hope to which he has called you, the riches of his glorious inheritance in the saints, and his incomparably great power for us who believe. (italics mine)

The connection between prayer and this spiritual episte- mology is unmistakable. This, again, affirms the role of God in this way of knowing. Psalm 25:14 shows that he is eager to "confide" in those who fear him. Many other psalms echo the sentiment of Psalm 119:18, which asks of God, "Open my eyes that I may see wonderful things in your law."

Often, it seems, this spiritual epistemology is actually in opposition to some of the other secular epistemologies. Colossians 2:8 speaks of "hollow and deceptive philosophy, which depends on human tradition and is based on the prin- ciples of this world rather than on Christ." Consider James's discussion of the contrast between worldly wisdom and the "wisdom that comes from heaven." Second Corinthians 10:3–5, however, shows most clearly the battle between earthly wisdom and that of "the knowledge of God":

> For though we live in the world, we do not wage war as the world does. The weapons we fight with are not the weapons of the world. On the contrary, they have divine power to demolish strongholds. We demolish arguments and every pre- tension that sets itself up against the knowledge of God, and we take captive every thought to make it obedient to Christ.

The church at Corinth, in fact, must have needed special instruction in the matter of this fifth epistemology. In Paul's first letter to the Corinthians he emphasized that the gospel he had delivered to them was never dependent on his preach- ing techniques: "I did not come with eloquence" (2:1); "not with wise and persuasive words" (2:4); not with "superior wisdom" (2:1) or "men's wisdom" (2:5). Instead, he stressed "a demonstration of the Spirit's power" and "God's power" (vv. 4, 5) as the epistemologies the Corinthians had received.

This "secret wisdom" (2:7) was one that is incomprehensible to others (vv. 7, 8) and accessible only through the Spirit:

> But God has revealed it to us by his Spirit. The Spirit searches all things, even the deep things of God. For who among men knows the thoughts of a man except the man's spirit within him? In the same way no one knows the thoughts of God except the Spirit of God. We have not received the spirit of the world but the Spirit who is from God, that we may understand what God has freely given us. This is what we speak, not in words taught us by human wisdom but in words taught by the Spirit, expressing spiritual truths in spiritual words. The man without the Spirit does not accept the things that come from the Spirit of God, for they are foolishness to him, and he cannot understand them, for they are spiritually discerned. The spiritual man makes judgments about all things, but he himself is not subject to any man's judgment:
>
> > "For who has known the mind of the Lord
> >   that he may instruct him?"
>
> But we have the mind of Christ.
>
> 1 Corinthians 2:10–16

The Power of the Unseen

Now, obviously this fifth epistemology is one that is not only unacknowledged by the world but is something the world cannot quantify or define, because it is outside the scope of the four epistemologies the world recognizes as being the only ways to know. This fifth epistemology is literally invisible to someone who does not recognize God's power, because such things are only "spiritually appraised" (1 Cor. 2:14 NAS).

Paul recognized two realms: the seen and the unseen. Just before he made the statement that Christians "live by faith, not by sight" (2 Cor. 5:7), he spoke of this unseen realm:

Therefore we do not lose heart. Though outwardly we are wasting away, yet inwardly we are being renewed day by day. For our light and momentary troubles are achieving for us an eternal glory that far outweighs them all. *So we fix our eyes not on what is seen, but on what is unseen.* For what is seen is temporary, but what is unseen is eternal.

2 Corinthians 4:16–17 (italics mine)

What is in this unseen realm? The writer of the Book of Hebrews directed our minds to something literally unseen but more real than anything we can touch: Jesus. In Hebrews 12:1 he urged believers to be aware of the "great cloud of witnesses" unseen by the world but whose influence can help us, and to be aware of and look toward Jesus (v. 2).

This awareness of the unseen realm makes everything different. The whole of life, instead of being a conglomeration of sometimes pointless skirmishes and goals, becomes a clearly delineated choice between operating on our own epistemologies and operating in accordance with the unseen realities that are more powerful than anything we touch around us.

Now, what has this to do with teaching someone who is a former Mormon?

I believe that many people who undertake to teach someone who has come out of a cult believe that they must make it a very meat-and-potatoes process, a no-frills indoctrination of Christianity that completely ignores the fifth epistemology of faith.

If you have not already thought of it this way, then perhaps you ought to consider that Christianity is anything *but* cut and dried. If you think otherwise, then try to sit down and, using any of the four secular epistemologies, explain or describe eternity. Or the Trinity. Or faith itself.

I smile when I see books that use the words *systematic* and *theology* in the same title. While it is true that most elements of Christianity are certainly transmittable through, say, authority or logic, some simply are not "packaged" that way.

Paul in 1 Corinthians chapter 1 addresses this issue. He said that worldly wisdom and intelligence, our purely secular epistemologies, are going to be destroyed by God. When the smoke clears at the end of time, it won't be our logic or our experiences that remain, but God's own brand of wisdom alone.

We have bought into the world's lie that the only things that are real are those things that we can measure or perceive with our senses. The measurable things of this world, far from being superior to the unseen realm, are actually far inferior to the realities of the fifth epistemology. Paul put it this way:

> But God chose the foolish things of the world to shame the wise; God chose the weak things of the world to shame the strong. He chose the lowly things of this world and the despised things—*and the things that are not*—to nullify the things that are, so that no one may boast before him.
>
> 1 Corinthians 1:27–29 (italics mine)

Many Christians, especially those from fundamentalist backgrounds, are afraid to address the issue of this unseen realm with someone who has come out of Mormonism. Sometimes they want to play it safe and just give 'em the facts, ma'am, just the four epistemology facts. Christians fear that ex-Mormons, whose former religion is so tightly circumscribed, will think they are not practical if they begin to tell them about the unseen realm.

I know that many of us are afraid to venture into talking about something that we cannot empirically or logically prove to the world. We are afraid of becoming like the people Paul described in Colossians 2:18:

> Do not let anyone who delights in false humility and the worship of angels disqualify you for the prize. Such a person goes

into great detail about what he has seen, and his unspiritual mind puffs him up with idle notions.

There is only one protection anyone has against this very real danger. Paul talked about this protection in the next verse when he warned against losing connection with "the Head, from whom the whole body, supported and held together by its ligaments and sinews, grows as God causes it to grow." The message is clear: All the focus must remain on the biblical Jesus Christ, not on our own experiences or perceptions.

Perhaps at this point it is necessary to make one thing clear. The epistemology of faith is not just for a "spiritual elite" or a certain strata of Christianity. Knowledge of original languages or scholarly study aids are not necessary for its operation in the mind of the believer. It is available to all peoples of all cultures and all times in history. Its only prerequisite is the desire to know God's will better.

Recognizing that spiritual insight is meant for all Christians will keep you from making the mistake of believing what all pseudo-Christian cults teach: that Scripture has "hidden" meanings that only a few can unlock or interpret.

Gordon Fee and Douglas Stuart in their terrific little book *How to Read the Bible for All Its Worth* (Zondervan, 1982) add a further caution for those who seek insight from Scripture so as to convey it to others. They say, "A text cannot mean what it never meant." In other words, everything written in the Bible had meaning for its original hearers or readers. No passage or idea has lain fallow and undiscovered until our day for one of us to have the only clue to its meaning. Recognizing this keeps the specters of pride and spiritual superiority at bay and also keeps us from going off on tangents that bear no relationship to the original meaning of any scriptural passage.

Now, that is not to say that God cannot give guidance for our individual situations through Scripture. It just means that it would be a great mistake to say that personal insight so obtained must be applied to all other situations, too. Here is an example. You have earnestly prayed for guidance in a decision about whether or not to move to Chicago and then decide you should move after you read a Scripture passage about being sent to a foreign land. This does not mean that the primary meaning of that particular passage as you teach it to your Sunday school class next week is that everyone there should move to Chicago.

Paul wrote about the dangers of the pride associated with people who claim "special knowledge" not available to other Christians:

> Now, brothers, I have applied these things to myself and Apollos for your benefit, so that you may learn from us the meaning of the saying, "Do not go beyond what is written." Then you will not take pride in one man over against another. For who makes you different from anyone else? What do you have that you did not receive? And if you did receive it, why do you boast as though you did not?
>
> 1 Corinthians 4:6–7

The Doubtful Value of the Practical

For some reason most Christians have gotten the idea that all our actions—and much of our theology—must be explainable according to strictly worldly standards. There are two reasons why the fear of speaking about the unseen realm with an ex-Mormon—for fear of being impractical—is not valid. First, Christianity is not a practical religion. *Practical* means that something works, according to the world's standards. If you have led someone out of Mormonism and promised that everything is going to go well for her because she made a decision for Christ, you have seriously misrepresented the Christian life. Hebrews chapter 12 and 1 Peter chapter 4 make it abundantly clear that God will allow the true Christian to be tested, and probably not in a pleasant way. Becoming a Christian is not a way to get rich (1 Tim. 6:5) or be popular (John 15:20) or have an easy life (2 Cor. 1:4.) It *is* a way to overcome, not evade, troubles in this life. It is a means to only one end: heaven.

Now, heaven is a supernatural place, and you cannot get there by natural means. If Jesus meant what he said in the Sermon on the Mount, you cannot even get there by practical means. You are stuck with relying on God, on his wisdom and on his ways, not on anything you can devise.

The second reason that you should not be afraid to discuss this unseen realm with an ex-Mormon is that she has already been living in a "spiritually aware state" if she was an active Mormon and knew that doctrine. You see, the Mormon Church teaches that each person has a spirit body that is the same size and shape as the physical body. At death, the physical body decays, but Mormons say this nearly tangible spirit body continues to live in the spirit world, which they identify as being located right here on earth. Every person who ever walked this earth in his or her physical body, in other words, continues to walk it in his or her spirit body, according to Mormon doctrine. As a faithful Mormon, I lived with the belief that every dead ancestor in my line back to Adam was observing me at all times. You talk about being spiritually aware; let me tell you about it! No Christian teaching about the overpowering reality of the unseen realm where God dwells would have shocked me. I just needed to have it *biblically* defined.

Anyone who has an interest in the power of awareness of the supernatural and its influence in Mormon history will benefit greatly from reading *Early Mormonism and the Magic World View* by Mormon scholar D. Michael Quinn (Signature Books, Salt Lake City, Utah, 1987). It is a revelation even to those of us who left Mormonism.

Now, one difficulty will undoubtedly arise as you begin to discuss unseen realities with an ex-Mormon. When you begin to show him there is a way of knowing that is beyond the four secular epistemologies, a way in which the unseen realities of God can be understood, he may experience some confusion. The question may be posed, "How is this any different from the things I took as confirmations when I was a Mormon, like the burning in the bosom, or experiences I had that seemed supernatural to me? How is this fifth epistemology any different from what I knew as a Mormon?"

You see, to a Mormon, the "final word" on ascertaining truth is a phenomenon known as "the burning in the bosom." According to *Doctrine and Covenants* 9:8–9, Joseph Smith was supposedly told in the process of translating the *Book of Mormon* by God that "you must study it out in your mind; then you must ask me [God] if it be right, and if it is right I [God] will cause that your bosom will burn within you; therefore, you shall feel that it is right. But if it is not right you shall have no such feelings, but you shall have such a stupor of thought that shall cause you to forget the thing which is wrong." This physical sensation is believed by Mormons to accompany all spiritual decision making, especially in the realm of discerning false doctrine from true.

This will be the time you can explain that God's wisdom can be communicated to us in more than one way. He can use the epistemology of authority (by transmitting the experiences of others as we read of them in the Bible). He can allow us to use our ability to logically deduce the meaning of Scriptures. He allows us to feel intuitive satisfaction in the Christian life, and he can use our own experiences of observing him in the created world to confirm his eternal power and divine nature.

However, these are also the epistemologies of our own minds and can operate, as we have seen, without our acknowledging God at all. The epistemology of intuition is especially independent, so to speak, for it needs only the human mind to operate; outside influences are purely optional. The only assurance we can have is of being led by God's Spirit, who 2 Corinthians 5:5 says is like a down payment or deposit that guarantees the unseen realities to come.

The ex-Mormon will understand this but will want to ask, "How can I know if I am being led by the Holy Spirit and not being deceived as I was before?" In other words, how can we differentiate intuition from the influence of the Holy Spirit?

As a Mormon, your friend carried a tremendous responsibility for determining the validity of anything he heard from his Mormon leaders. A former prophet of the LDS church, Harold B. Lee, once stated: "We can know, or have the assurance that they [Mormon leaders] are speaking under inspiration if we so live that we can have a witness that what they are speaking is the word of the Lord. There is only one safety, and that is that we shall live to have the witness to know." Thus any assessment of truth was based on (1) one's own goodness (and which of us can ever know when we are good enough?) and (2) the subsequent subjective feelings (intuition).

Never, of course, does the Bible advocate that anyone test doctrine against his own life nor against feelings.

The comforting answer to the ex-Mormon's question about how to assess truth is found in John 16:13, where the Holy Spirit is called the "Spirit of truth" who "will guide you into all truth."

So how do we know if we are being led into truth?

We must take God seriously when he tells us that all Scripture is breathed by him and is useful and is the standard for correcting error (2 Tim. 3:16). So if we wonder if we are being led by the Spirit, we should not look to our own goodness nor to our feelings about something. We should instead look to where we end up: our conclusions must square with divinely revealed truth in the Bible.

Mormonism is not truth, because it conflicts with the Bible. Therefore, one cannot be led into it by the Holy Spirit, because only he leads people into truth.

Any new perception must harmonize with what the Bible says, for "God is not a God of disorder but of peace" (1 Cor. 14:33). Any subjective feelings we have that lead us anywhere other than into truth could not be from God. They must have some other source.

Symbolism and Contrast: Tools of the Fifth Epistemology

For we know in part, and we prophesy in part; but when the perfect comes, the partial will be done away.

When I was a child, I used to speak as a child, think as a child, reason as a child; when I became a man, I did away with childish things.

For now we see in a mirror dimly, but then face to face; now I know in part, but then I shall know fully just as I also have been fully known.

—1 Corinthians 13:9–13 NAS (italics mine)

Two books of the New Testament completely overwhelm me with their emphasis on the unseen: Ephesians and Hebrews. In the opening verses of Ephesians, Paul pointedly places the setting of his teachings outside of earth time: "before the creation of the world" (1:4) and in the context of "the heavenly realms" (1:3; 1:20; 2:6; 3:10; 6:12). He jars us out of earthly thinking and reasoning with image after image that arrests and reforms our thinking processes: deposits, power, walls, citizenship, house construction, mystery, body, light and darkness. Then he delivers the knock-out punch to our minds. He shows us two images that explain everything he has said before, two images that portray all the unseen realities. He shows us that our relationships with each other (husbands with wives, children with parents, and slaves with masters) are visible realities of our relationship with God. Then Paul rips away the veil of our understanding and lets us see right into the raging battlefield of the unseen.

The Book of Hebrews uses a little different tack to get us to see the unseen realities. Its writer carefully contrasts everything his Jewish audience knows (from their four earthly epistemologies) with the ultimate reality—Jesus. The writer uses the modes of revelation (angelic authority, Moses, high priests, Melchizedek, covenants, the tabernacle, law, and sacrifices) to show what those things had once meant to the Jewish mind, then uses them to show how they found realization in the person of Jesus Christ.

Each of these things, as is said specifically of the law in Hebrews 10:1, is "only a shadow of the good things that are coming—not the realities themselves." Like the sacrifices in verse 3, they are only "reminders." They point, as the writer so aptly observes, to a new-covenant time when, God promises, "I will put my laws in their hearts, and I will write them on their minds" (v. 16).

Then comes the great chapter on faith. All the stories that follow, of great people who operated on faith, are built on verse 2 of chapter 11, which tells us flatly that all of history is anchored in two principles: Everything in existence came into being at the direct operation of God's word, and "what is seen was not made out of what was visible" (v. 3). *The unseen, then, far from being just an embellishment to faith, is, instead, its very foundation.*

The writer then goes on to show how the compelling power of unseen realities (only revealed to us through God's Word) have dictated the actions of the great people of history. These people were indeed informed at times by earthly epistemologies. They saw the walls of Jericho fall (empiricism), heard the spoken blessings of Isaac, Jacob, and Joseph when each was an old man (authority), assessed situations and reasoned about what God could or could not do in a hard situation (reason), and "longed for a better country" (subjective feelings). Yet these sources of information did not make the people great. What makes them heroes of faith is the way they responded to the unseen realities that kept them going.

The writer of Hebrews anchored faith firmly in the unseen when he told his readers that they were surrounded by an invisible "great cloud of witnesses." Far from telling them to use earthly epistemologies to assess their situations, he advised them to "fix their eyes" on Jesus (who is undeniably invisible to our earthly senses). He told them flatly, "You have not come to a mountain that can be touched" (Heb. 12:18) but to a heavenly mountain of the unseen, and then cautioned:

> See to it that you do not refuse him who speaks. If they did not escape when they refused him who warned them on earth, how much less will we, if we turn away from him who warns us from heaven?
>
> Hebrews 12:25

And none of us wants to refuse him. We want to listen, to tune our ears to receive what he has to say.

Symbolism in the Old Testament

Throughout history, God has used a special tool of his own epistemology to convey truth to his people, the tool of symbolism. This is something far beyond (while by no means exclusive of) type and antitype. In type and antitype, one earthly thing (usually a person, such as Moses) prefigures another future earthly reality in Scripture (such as Christ). However, I will use symbolism in a broader sense, where an earthly reality (person, situation, object) is used to reveal to the believer's mind a spiritual reality that exists in the mind of God or in eternity.

Symbolism as a means to convey understanding is seen throughout the Old Testament, but God most overtly used this teaching tool through the agency of the prophets.

When Jeremiah was called to be a prophet, his first objection was that he was "only a child" and did not know *how* to speak to the people God was calling him to address. After touching Jeremiah's mouth with his hand, God announced, "Now I have put my words into your mouth" (Jer. 1:9). What immediately followed was not a treatise on the sins of the people nor a list of reforms that God wanted. Instead, God showed Jeremiah two symbols and identified their meanings: an almond tree branch, signifying that God would watch to see that his word was fulfilled, and a boiling pot that represented the destruction that would soon be poured out in judgment.

Throughout his life Jeremiah combined direct predictions of coming disasters with physical images to arrest the worldly thinking of his listeners, to startle them into some action. Jeremiah was told to buy a linen belt, wear it for a while, and then bury it. When he dug it up later, he was told that it was a symbol of how ruined and useless the idolatrous nation of Israel was, even though it had, like the belt, been bound close to its owner, God. Later God used the setting of a potter's workshop to show that he, like the potter, was sovereign over his own creations. Two baskets of figs represented exiles; some good, some worthless. Jeremiah even publicly wore a wooden and leather yoke to demonstrate coming captivity, bought a field to demonstrate coming redemption, dictated words on a scroll whose message was so powerful that the king tried to annul it by burning it. The people's hearts were cauterized by sin and, beyond all words, these images etched into those flinty surfaces the urgent demand for repentance.

Ezekiel, too, was commanded by God to do symbolic things to try to shake his hearers into a comprehension that words alone were incapable of bringing. Having been called to prophesy by a magnificent vision that was itself a symbol of God's brilliance and multifaceted attributes, Ezekiel carried the marks of that unforgettable experience into his own ministry.

I wonder what the people who watched him thought as they observed him putting siege ramps up against a model of the city of Jerusalem, or lying for 390 days on one side and then forty days on the other while subsisting on rations of water and a strange, amalgamated bread, or shaving his beard and weighing out part of the hairs to burn, part to strike with a sword, part to scatter to the wind, and part to tuck in his garment.

Then, most dreadful of all, Ezekiel himself became a symbol to the people of Israel of the otherwise incomprehensible horror that awaited their continued disobedience (4:14–17).

Even now, thousands of year later, though I may not remember all I have read that Ezekiel said, I will never be able to erase from my mind even that which my physical eyes never saw, but that which my mind will always retain: a man furtively carrying his belongings in a bundle, squeezing through a jabbed out hole in Jerusalem's wall; someone holding two sticks aloft in one hand and explaining coming unity to an incredulous audience; a mourner whose only delight—his wife—is taken from him as the ultimate symbol of loss while he is forbidden to shed a single tear.

Through such devices God has continued to "actualize" with physical objects those things that are not physical but are nonetheless very real. The symbols of Jeremiah and Ezekiel, for instance, made real to observers what was already a reality to God's mind: the future. Just because it was not tangible or apprehensible by the four earthly epistemologies did not mean that it did not exist in God's ultimate reality.

It is difficult for the human mind to grasp the fact that there can be a reality beyond that which we experience. We state facts and do not know how to handle other "facts" that do not fit. For instance, we might say unequivocally, "July is a hot month." We stand outside in hundred-degree heat and know that is a fact. But what do we do when someone arrives in Phoenix, Arizona, on July 22 on an airplane from Tierra del Fuego carrying an ice chest full of freshly fallen snow? We admit that elsewhere there can be another equally valid reality.

The ultimate symbol of that heavenly reality, of course, was the person of Jesus Christ. He is the imported snow on our faces that cools us, that negates and changes the effect of the worldly heat around us. And the Bible encourages us to look at the realities he taught not as *equally* valid with our experiences but as *superior*. We should not be surprised, when we look at the way he conveyed information to people, that he, too, used this fifth epistemology of faith and used it in two distinct ways.

Jesus' Use of the Fifth Epistemology

The first tool of the fifth epistemology Jesus used (even ahead of symbolism) was contrast. His divinely ordained precursor, John the Baptist, was himself a visible, jarring contrast to the society around him—someone who did not eat what they ate, wear what they wore, live where they lived, or say what they said. This man came according to prophecy to straighten out the crooked and smooth out the rough. His message, in fact, was to tell people to turn their backs on old ways: to repent.

It was into this atmosphere of friction between realities that Jesus began to teach. His very first words in the Sermon on the Mount were words that rubbed against each other, concepts that did not add up in earthly ways, near paradoxes that must be explained, juxtapositions of "you have heard it said" of their earthly epistemologies against "I tell you." Far from negating the Jews' epistemology of the authority of their Scriptures, he reaffirmed even jots and tittles while showing his listeners that there was something more to be apprehended.

The results were astounding. Matthew's account of the Sermon on the Mount ends with the observation that Jesus' listeners were amazed at what he had taught, because his teachings carried a new kind of weight of truth to them. They rang true, not because they squared with the past experiences of the hearers but because they penetrated to where the cut-and-dried instructions of the teachers of the law could never reach—their souls.

What this tool of contrast did, in fact, was to break connections in the minds of the hearers, causing them to question what they thought they knew, to jettison illegitimate notions from the past. Look at how Jesus did this, over and over, in the Sermon on the Mount. He tackled everyday situations (divorce, oaths, revenge, prayer, physical needs), appealed to his listeners to recall the principles with which they had assessed these situations, and then told them, in effect, "Forget the way you previously understood this, and take another look at how to handle it."

The second tool of the spiritual epistemology that Jesus used was the metaphoric language of symbols. At first, it was often incomprehensible even to his disciples. John records in chapter 6 of his Gospel that after Jesus fed the five thousand men and then told them that he was himself the true bread, many of them grumbled, saying, "This is a hard teaching" (v. 60). Jesus then identified the words he had delivered to them as being spirit (verse 63), accessible only through an enabling Father. As a result, many of his disciples turned away from him forever (v. 66), but Peter summarized their dilemma: There was nowhere else they could go for these words of eternal life.

Parables, too, presented a problem. For some, they provided exponential understanding (Matt. 13:12). Others, however, who did not have the seeds of understanding, Jesus said, would understand even less as they went along in life.

For those who could understand, Jesus used symbols and metaphors to their fullest extent. No amount of straight exposition on the active love of God, for instance, can begin to match the impact of the story of a woman sweeping her floor by candlelight to find her lost coin, which was probably part of her dowry; or the story of a man penning ninety-nine sheep so he can look for one lost one; or the image of a father whose watching eyes see from a distance the son he had loved and lost. Such mental pictures assault our senses and minds even today in a way that no instruction ever could, then leave us, somewhat residually, with something far more durable than anything we have learned another way.

When I look in a panoramic manner at the way Jesus taught people, it seems to me that, while he used the tool of contrast to break down old, false conceptions in the minds of his hearers, he used symbolism to reestablish a connection with the heavenly realities to which they had been previously blinded. "Blessed are your eyes because they see," he told his disciples while he discussed his use of parables, "and your ears because they hear" (Matt. 13:16).

Contrast in Our Teaching

The people to whom Jesus spoke were deeply immersed in secular culture and its influence on their thinking. I find several things to be learned from the way he taught them. First, he did work through some of their secular epistemologies to teach them (primarily through the authority epistemology, but also sometimes through reason and empiricism), but his teaching was no mere rehashing of things they knew or even had prior access to. He awakened the fifth epistemology of faith in them, which made his teaching different from what they had previously experienced. It caused some people to be threatened and some to be delighted (Luke 13:17).

Now, if the master teacher could use these two tools, contrast and symbolism, to help blinded people begin to see, surely we may use them also.

We must bear in mind that it is God who gives this special, Spirit-empowered understanding. Contrast jolts us into a new way of seeing; symbolism broadens our field of vision and links us with the communication devices of heaven. But they are ever God's domain into which he invites us. We can only court the Spirit through such things as contrast and symbolism; we do not control him.

It is important when using these two elements of the fifth epistemology of faith that we as teachers recognize that the tools themselves are not the end result. In other words, creating contrasts that will cause a person to think in new ways is not an end in itself. Nor is identifying a symbol and its meaning just a goal. Both of these, as used by Jesus, had a result that was beyond the individual elements: the enlightenment of the mind by the Holy Spirit.

Of course, there are inherent dangers. Without the checks and balances of biblical truth, there can be uncertainty. (Is this just my own mind operating—intuition—or is this from the Lord?) That is why there is absolutely no substitute for spending devoted, quality time reading Scripture, for teacher and student alike. You cannot know if an insight fits with biblical truth if you don't read the Bible.

Let's look at how the tool of contrast can be used in a teaching situation with an ex-Mormon. Contrast occurs when a concept new to the mind of the ex-Mormon is rubbed up against one of his old preconceptions. The spark of insight produced from the friction of ideas is not valuable only for its experience (empiricism), nor can it be quantified only as the absorption of the new information (authority), nor is it just the feeling of discomfort it produces (intuition), nor is it even an assessment alone of how it fits into previous thoughts (reason). It is ultimately a medium through which the Holy Spirit communicates, a sort of holy "Aha!"

The specific situation in which contrast is most significantly used in teaching an ex-Mormon is to juxtapose Mormon doctrine (either as recalled by the ex-Mormon, or documented from LDS doctrinal sources) up against Bible truth. But that's not too original, you might say; people have been doing that for years.

I saw this clearly illustrated by the seven other people who contributed to my book *Why We Left Mormonism* (Baker Book House, 1990). Each person had come into contact with a fact or idea that challenged (or, more commonly, contradicted) what they thought they knew from their Mormon worldview. I found it truly significant that for each of us who had left Mormonism, the jarring information that led us to that action was different in each case. What shocked one Mormon apparently left the others unperturbed. This emphasized to me the fact that you should never rely on any one method of trying to reach someone in a cult but, instead, try to find out what is important to the individual and then lovingly contrast his or her cultic information on that particular point to what the Bible teaches that opposes it.

Symbolism in Our Teaching

I believe that contrast alone, while it produces the jarring rethinking of past error, does not retie the mind solidly. That is where symbolism comes in.

You may have noticed that up until now this book has used the tool of contrast to open up the mind of you, the reader. Recall how I described in detail the four epistemologies that the world says are the only ways we learn. In the chapter that followed, I gave successive Scripture references to show that the Bible teaches another, additional epistemology. I repeatedly rubbed it up against the four epistemologies to show you the differences.

I would be willing to bet that the friction there created a spark of understanding in you that was not there other times you may have read those Scripture passages. (I apologize to those of you who for years have seen this fifth epistemology without my help. My experience with most Christians, however, is that they have been taught to identify it only as subjective response, thus robbing the Holy Spirit of his due in this matter.)

The tool of symbolism is trickier to use with an ex-Mormon. However, whereas contrast breaks connections with old ideas, there is a great need for something to reconnect the mind to those unseen but supremely valid realities that are beyond our four secular epistemologies: those things that are true and tangible in eternity. They *are* eternity, distilled and extruded through the pores of our insensate world, and biblical symbols are the means of understanding them.

It has helped me to think of things this way. When the Bible speaks in 1 Corinthians of our seeing things as through a mirror dimly, I have let my mind meditate on the concept that God sees us clearly, but we are not able to view him in the same way. It is as if God has covered the world with a thick film that is like a two-way mirror through which he can see but we cannot.

As he looks on the earth, he sees it very differently than we do. He doesn't see map lines of the boundaries of countries. Political movements and revolutions that are front-page news because of their scope are viewed by him only one soul at a time. He does not measure progress by expanding frontiers or inventions. Only one thing matters to him as he looks down: how many faces he can see that are raised toward him and not looking down at the dirt beneath our feet.

Beyond our view are invisible structures, as the Book of Ephesians teaches, that literally support this world and all its workings. Our created energies, even the power of gravity itself, all pale in comparison with the active power that raised Jesus from the dead: a power only comprehensible through the Spirit's own epistemology and invisible to those who refuse him.

Occasionally throughout history God has literally pushed objects through this film from his realm into ours. An example of this is manna. When the Israelite people put those sweet flakes into their mouths, they were eating eternity—something that came from God. God expected them to see it that way and to regard that reality of his providence as being *more real* than the barren desert that surrounded them.

In Daniel 5, the hand of God pushed through this film and became visible to men who watched it write a warning onto the wall. This was reality—the future as God knew it would happen—that invaded our world.

The miracles Jesus performed were never intended by him to be seen as ends in themselves. A healing, for instance, was to picture the way things are *supposed* to be—how they will be in eternity. But more important, his miracles were symbols of God's power and love that were to awaken faith as they confirmed the truth of what he taught.

Jesus insisted that certain symbols he used not be considered coequal with other visible realities. When he talked of the communion, he urged Christians to eat bread that he identified as his own body. Surely the disciples must have been startled to hear him say that, just as they had been in the synagogue of Capernaum when he had told them pointedly that his flesh was "real food" and his blood, "real drink."

Thus, when I raise the communion bread and wine to my lips, I tremble. To me, they have been pushed through this film in the same way manna was. They are the most real things in the room. When I swallow them, I ingest eternity.

Another aspect of such a symbol is that, like many other great symbols of the Bible, through it Jesus invites our participation in it. He ties us to himself through such symbols.

The baptismal waters are not just observed, they flow over us. The communion bread and wine enter our bodies. Praise pours from our throats.

The most overt, unmistakable symbol ever pushed through our film of blindness, though, is the person of Jesus. He is the ultimate meaning. How wonderful that he allows participation with himself, too! He does not just dwell within us (though that would be enough). He allows us to be clothed with him (Gal. 3:27) and to relive the most dramatic experience of his life as we, too, die, are buried, and raised with him in baptism (Rom. 6:4).

7

Tainted Symbols

For the message of the cross is foolishness to those
who are perishing, but to us who are being saved it is
the power of God.

—1 Corinthians 1:18

An awakening understanding of a symbol has many
similarities to pregnancy. (Male readers: Great prophets of
the Bible—Jesus included—used childbirth analogies freely,
so I have precedence here.)

Symbolism, as I described it in the last chapter, involves
elements of another presence that intrudes into our physical
world. At first, we feel just tiny flutterings of understanding,
and though we know they mean something, we wonder if
we just imagine the other presence. So we seek corrobora-
tion, and another, stronger movement is felt. Soon the presence is unmistakable. Before long, its influence takes over
our lives.

I believe that symbols *themselves* are representations of
God's condescension to the human mind. They meet our

very human need to *see* something, making aspects of our faith literally tangible to our five senses. Like Thomas who refused to believe until he touched, we, too, need contact with God, and symbols provide that.

Throughout history, God has been concerned about how symbols represented him. After he told the nation of Israel that they were going to be the symbol of how he would deal with people he called for his purpose, they often appealed to his sensitivity about his "image" before the other nations. They would often ask him to get them out of trouble, saying, in effect, that he had a good reputation to protect by taking care of them. (Psalm 79 is a good example of this.)

Once, when King Ahab was being attacked by the Arameans, those enemies thought they could easily defeat the Israelites if they fought them in a valley. A man of God relayed God's words to Ahab: "Because the Arameans think the LORD is a god of the hills and not a god of the valleys, I will deliver this vast army into your hands, and you will know that I am the LORD" (1 Kings 20:28).

Later, God ordained tongues as a sign for unbelievers (not believers), reasoning that people who came into God's assemblies would draw certain conclusions based on what they saw represented there (1 Cor. 14:22–25).

God has always been very sensitive about how he is portrayed by us and how that portrait is conveyed to others. Our faith, like Abraham's, is made complete by our actions, and even our conduct reflects on God.

As you begin to use symbols as a teaching tool, consider that there is no more powerful symbol on this earth than the church itself. Nowhere else is God's power in this world more visibly manifest, as body parts follow the lead of a divine head.

Jesus recognized the power of symbols and willingly submitted himself to them. He who was the embodiment of covenant was subjected to circumcision. He who was without sin allowed himself to be baptized. Jesus, the great High Priest, worshiped at the temple, mingling with the best and the worst of humanity, outside the curtain of the Holy of Holies where he alone should have been able to enter unhindered.

Tracing the Taint

Now, if the great symbols of the Bible are indeed inherently imbued with such power, it would seem to make sense to tap into this power by appealing to an ex-Mormon's fifth epistemology with the great symbols of the Bible. However, this is not the case, at least not at first.

The problem is that each of the great symbols of the Bible —those things that carry the significance of eternity with them—have been tainted in Mormonism. Many examples exist, but I will deal with only a few specifically. You in your study undoubtedly will uncover more.

The first symbol is baptism. The Bible says it is to signify salvation and cleansing and identification with Jesus in his death, burial, and resurrection. But consider what the ex-Mormon's epistemology of empiricism taught him. All children of eight years of age are baptized, because Mormon doctrine teaches that this is the age at which people become accountable for their sins. Since baptism and accountability coincide, Mormon baptism of children is inherently a preventative measure, something like a scheduled inoculation.

Nor is baptism the personal, individual matter we know. It can, in fact, be done in proxy for someone who never during earth life repented of sin. Thus, instead of being an identification with the living Christ, vicarious baptism is, by definition, identification with someone who is dead.

A second earthly symbol that Mormonism will have corrupted in the mind of an ex-Mormon is the concept of the church itself. Mormons don't think of the church as a symbol at all. It is a very solid, earthbound hierarchal empire of General Authorities at the head, local officials in the middle, and regular people at the base.

How differently the Bible portrays the church! First Corinthians chapter 12 and Ephesians chapter 4 use the symbol of a living, moving body of absolutely coequal parts to help us see our relationship to the headship of Christ. Ephesians 5 uses the picture of a loving, supportive, protective husband whose wife willingly submits to his health-giving direction. Imagine the incongruity of such things to a Mormon-trained mind that "knows" the church is a corporation!

The symbolism of giving is another symbol that has been stripped of meaning by Mormon doctrine and practice. The Bible teaches that the act of contributing to the needs of God's church is an act that unleashes all sorts of powers. Second Corinthians chapter 9 tells us that through the church God works to meet *our own* financial needs so that we can continue to give. In addition, such giving is a mechanism to activate the prayers of others in our behalf. When we Christians give, we take something physical and tangible and release it into the world of the unseen where it can work and act under God's direction. By releasing our hold on money we become rich in many other ways as well.

Contrast this to the way that a Mormon is taught to give. Far from being the anonymous action we know, a Mormon giving is to put money in an envelope with his name and the specific fund to which he wants the money given checked. At the end of each calendar year, a faithful Mormon attends "tithing settlement" with a church official and must be able to document the fact that he has given at least ten percent of his income. (Some estimates of the amount of money that the different obligations require puts the actual annual percentage nearer one-fourth of an active Mormon's gross income.)

The cost of not paying can be high. A Mormon who does not contribute the amount required cannot, for instance, attend services of any sort in the temple—a stiff social penalty to the Mormon.

Thus, giving is not the release of worldly things into the uncontrolled (by the individual) realm of the unseen; the

Mormon requirement to give is a very real tool to control, manipulate, and punish people that is used by the church.

Other symbols corrupted by Mormon doctrine have to do with the concepts of priesthood and temple imagery.

The Book of Hebrews powerfully advances the idea that the old Jewish concept of priesthood had been done away with in the new covenant, because now we have the perfect High Priest, Jesus. Through this has been instituted a tremendous leveling of humanity, with Jesus alone standing above to intercede for us at the ultimate Holy of Holies. Like the high priests of old, he who was called by God offers gifts and sacrifices for our sins (Heb. 5:1).

Instead of just one high priest, Mormonism has literally thousands of humans who wear that title. Very much unlike the Jewish high priest who represented men before God, Mormon high priests claim to represent God before men: theology upside down.

In addition, all temple imagery in the Bible is virtually incomprehensible to the Mormon mind, because it bears absolutely no resemblance to LDS temples. The Old Testament temple was a bustling place of smoke and incense and the smells and sounds of animals being sacrificed. There, atonement was made.

A Mormon temple is antiseptic gold and white, the setting for baptisms for the dead and spray-nozzle washings and cinematic dramas leading up to weddings and curse-laden ceremonies they call "endowments." There, they believe, gods are made.

The Bible makes it very clear that we are to look carefully at all the elements of the temple, from its purpose to its furnishings to its ordinances. Far from being outmoded because they are no longer in earthly existence, we are told, all these elements are significant because that sanctuary was "a copy and shadow of what is in heaven" (Heb. 8:5), sort of a spiritual blueprint we cannot just ignore or modify or abandon.

But one of the most powerful symbols of all Christianity is not only misapprehended by the Mormon mind but actually despised by it. It is the symbol, most precious to the Christian mind, of the cross.

No cross of any sort adorns any Mormon meeting house, indoors or out. It is not used on Bibles or hymnbooks. Like all my Mormon friends, I refused to wear a crucifix as jewelry. The idea was repugnant to me. Why would I want to wear an instrument of torture around my neck? Any reference to it seemed parochial and backward. I chose to see Christ teaching, feeding the five thousand, walking along roads, resurrected—any way except on the cross.

That was because Mormon doctrine had taught me that the atonement of Christ had taken place not on the cross but hours before in the Garden of Gethsemane. All the blood and messiness of the cross seemed anticlimactic, any portrayal of it an appeal to emotion. Added to all that, I believed Mormon doctrine that stated that Christ's atonement itself had only one result: People (all people) would be resurrected, not united with Christ but only raised from the dead to face judgment where each one's individual deeds would determine a "degree of glory." The cross, therefore, was just a shameful interim between atonement in the garden and my chance to prove I was worthy to go to the celestial kingdom. As a Mormon, I completely embodied 1 Corinthians 1:18–25:

> For the message of the cross is foolishness to those who are perishing, but to us who are being saved it is the power of God . . . we preach Christ crucified: a stumbling block to Jews and foolishness to Gentiles, but to those God has called, both Jews and Greeks, Christ the power of God and the wisdom of God.
>
> 1 Corinthians 1:18, 23–24

Now here is the point in teaching a former Mormon: You cannot start with the symbols, because you will probably be trying to access an image in the mind of the ex-Mormon that bears no similarity to the heavenly reality it is supposed to portray. Especially in the area of symbols, which have been corrupted and misused by Mormonism, contrast must precede use of the symbol.

The Narrow Road of Symbolism Use

The temptation will be strong to use earthbound symbols to get a point across rather than to correct the corrupted ones. There are two reasons why you must resist this temptation. First, if you "invent" an earthly symbol (say, for instance, use a computer metaphor to try to explain the workings of the mind of God), you cut yourself off from the connection to the heavenly realities inherent in God's own symbols. The second reason is that God has surely foreseen that his symbols would be corrupted and has made provisions for faithful teachers to overcome this.

There are scriptural warnings against using what I would call human pseudo symbols that purport to represent the unseen. An example of this is found in 1 Timothy 1:3, where Paul advised Timothy to "command certain men not to teach false doctrines any longer nor to devote themselves to myths and endless genealogies." Paul went on to explain that the results of such teachings were controversies that would diminish God's work, "which is by faith."

Nor should emphasis on a symbol be allowed to supplant or overshadow the meaning of the unseen reality it represents. Though the temple was very important to the Jews, Jeremiah carried this message to them: "Do not trust in deceptive words and say, 'This is the temple of the LORD, the temple of the LORD!'" (Jer. 7:4). He went on to say that just appealing to the symbol was useless if the Jews did not bring their wicked actions under control and quit trusting in the holiness of a building to save their cheating skins. Jesus

repeated the same sentiment in Matthew 23:16–17 when he
questioned the Jews' thinking that the gold of the temple
was holier than the temple that sanctified it.

C. S. Lewis had some interesting insights on the use of
biblical images. In *Letters to Malcolm* he advised: "When the
purport of the images—what they say to our fear, and hope,
and will, and affections—seems to conflict with the theological abstractions, trust the purport of the images every
time. For our abstract thinking is itself a tissue of analogies:
a continual modeling of spiritual reality in legal, or chemi-
cal, or mechanical terms. Are these likely to be more ade-
quate than the sensuous, organic, and personal images of
Scripture—light and darkness, river and well, father and child?
The footprints of the Divine are more visible in that rich soil
than across rocks or slag heaps."

The Process of Demythologizing Error

A former Catholic will not be able to visualize himself as
a *saint* because of the way this word was appropriated by his
old church. Mormons have similar problems. Much of the
powerful language of the Bible has been neutralized in cultic teaching. Peter's teachings about making "your calling
and election sure" may be interesting to the average Christian, but they hardly bear the emotional wallop they would
for a Mormon who believes this is a mystical experience of
communication with God. Be sensitive to facial expressions
and be very apt to let your ex-Mormon friend tell you when
certain phrases of Scripture are carrying excess baggage from
LDS days. Doing word studies of the individual words, looking up other places where the Greek words appear in the
Bible, and consulting several translations can all be used to
rub up against the preconceptions.

It is good to bear in mind that the Mormon comes to
Christianity with a full panoply of cultic symbols of his own.

He sat for years in the pew singing, "Praise to the Man" (about Joseph Smith) and "We Thank Thee Oh God for a Prophet" (about the corporation's president) and "I Am a Child of God" (about preexistence and future godhood). Be prepared, when discussing Christian symbolism with your ex-Mormon friend, to listen sympathetically and kindly as he discusses what still may be cherished things. Then gently, as the opportunity presents itself and the Spirit directs, use contrasting biblical symbols to rub up against them and produce those sparks of insight that will allow him to throw those false idols over his shoulder as he runs away from them for refuge (Isa. 2:19–22).

It seems almost silly to me to have to remind you that something as inherently powerful as a biblical symbol can be grossly misused. Like any great tool, it can be rendered worthless when used for shock value or personal gain. If you have ever doubted this, look no further than Robert Mapplethorpe's picture of a crucifix immersed in urine. No amount of thinking about the entrance of salvation into a filthy world could ever justify such abuse of a godly symbol.

Some Closing Caveats

We might also expect some of the less desirable results that Jesus himself experienced when he used the tools of contrast and symbolism. First of all, not everyone will listen to the truths of the gospel. As the parable of the sower shows, not everyone who receives the word and lets it begin to grow will follow through and produce a crop. Of those who do listen, many, like the rich young man of Matthew 19, will let other considerations keep them from following through on what they hear. We might also expect the criticism and alienation from people like the Pharisees who refuse to sanction anything that is not done the old-fashioned way, the way *they* have always taught.

The use of contrast and symbolism are not surefire. They are tools of the Spirit, and he does not always act in completely predictable ways in the lives of those he owns (John 3:6–8). As with any gifts of the Spirit, we should recognize and activate contrast and symbolism, not manipulate them.

Part 3

The Teaching: Assessment, Contrast, and Symbolism

The purposes of man's heart are deep waters, but a man of understanding draws them out.

—Proverbs 20:5

How to Use This Section

Despite all that I have emphasized up to this point about the fact that activating our fifth epistemology is not a one-two-three process because it is Spirit controlled, I nonetheless believe strongly that guidance by a Christian is essential for the new ex-Mormon believer. I have chosen four major areas in which such a new believer needs instruction: the Godhead, salvation and the church, the role of Scripture, and obedience and trust in others.

Though all the specific teaching in this book deals with Mormon doctrine, I believe that the method this book outlines is applicable to other cults too. Worldview assessment, tracking down the epistemologies of the ex-cultist, Scripture contrast and symbolism—all are certainly "do-able" in the context of any cult. Information on specific cults, including Scripture passages that contrast with cultic teaching, is available through your local Christian bookstore. If you are teaching an ex-Jehovah's Witness, an ex-Christian Scientist, or someone who has left New Age teaching, I suggest that you avail yourself of the information and insights of the ex-cultists interviewed in *Why We Left A Cult: Six People Tell Their Stories* (Baker Book House, 1992). Of particular value to your study would be the books and publications these six people recommend as being effective and accurate.

In keeping with the things discussed previously, in the lesson format you will do the following with each subject:

Pray with the student (establish a spiritual commonality and let him see spirituality in action).

Assess the subject's role in the student's worldview (ask questions I will provide so you can understand his presuppositions and apprehend how he uses terminology).

Determine by which epistemology he came to his knowledge (again, using questions I will provide).

Contrast Mormon doctrinal statements with the Bible (rubbing them up against each other for the spark of insight as well as for the information).

Avail yourself of insight by *reading* pertinent passages in more than one Bible translation. (I suggest the New International Version, King James Version, and New American Standard Version.)

Share insights from the previous week's personal Bible reading and prayer (a time for sharing on a spiritual basis as well as an opportunity for you to be able to guide the student if he gets off course because he operates on false presuppositions).

It is most important during the contrast part of the lesson, where LDS teaching is compared with the Bible, to continually encourage the student to spend private time looking up the Scriptures and reading the entire chapter (or more) that surrounds a passage. Usually thoughts are tied inherently to what came before and goes after the reading. Context is a major part of understanding, and it is only in the interest of limited lesson time that I have quoted parts of Scripture which, like diamonds, really need their settings to shine.

Of course, the worldview and contrast questions from here on will be useless to you if you have not digested the first part of this book.

One further note: Encourage the student to keep a small notebook in which he writes down Scripture passages that are helpful or illuminating to him, as well as questions that arise as he reads Scripture or meditates on it.

God be with you!

Lesson 1

Redefining the Godhead (Assessment)

Preparation

Pray together that God will show himself to you through Scripture. Read together the following Scripture verses and discuss together what they promise: John 17:3; Ephesians 1:17.

Worldview Assumptions

To begin to appreciate the student's worldview, ask the following questions to determine her presuppositions. Be sympathetic and understanding when there is confusion in her mind. Do not attempt to correct or teach at this point. Write down major points the student makes, especially the source of her presuppositions if she mentions them.

How would you describe God to someone from a totally different culture?

In which specific ways can God affect or control the life of a believer?

Does God have a past? Describe what you know about it. Did he have a beginning in time?

In which ways are God and humans alike? In which ways are they different?

What is the relationship of God to Jesus Christ?

Who or what is the Holy Spirit?

In what ways are God the Father, Jesus, and the Holy Spirit one? In what ways are they separate?

Are there any laws or principles to which God is subject?

Epistemologies

To determine how the student came to her conclusions about God, ask the following questions. Again, write down her responses, encourage without prompting, and be loving and nonjudgmental when what she says may contradict the Bible.

What is your earliest memory of God?

What did you believe about God during your preteen years?

What did you believe about God during your teens and as a young adult? Who taught you most about God? What specifics do you remember?

In which ways did you believe that what you were taught about God (or experienced about him) was confirmed by events in your life?

Looking back, would you say you got most of your information about what God is like from your own observations, from reading or being taught, by reasoning things out, or from the feelings that you had about him? Give an example of the way you learned about him most effectively.

Assignment for Home Study

Both you and the student should commit yourselves to earnest prayer for insight and guidance during the coming days that precede your next meeting. You both also will promise to look up the following passages: John chapters 14, 15, 16, and 17. Encourage the student to read the passages at one sitting several times during the coming days.

Redefining the Godhead
(Contrast and Symbolism)

Preparation

Review the homework passages from the last session. Read the passages aloud in at least one version other than the one the student used, and ask the student: "What general impression about the Godhead, do you think, does this Scripture passage give? What have you learned about God that you did not know before?"

Contrast (Introduction)

Ask the worldview and epistemology questions from the previous session. Of course, these are just starter questions; you will probably think of some yourself as the conversation progresses. By now you should have a good idea of which epistemology or epistemologies seemed most important to the student in the past concerning this particular subject. (Chances are with doctrinal matters such as the Godhead, he got most of his information from the authority epistemology of being taught.)

The LDS doctrinal statements that follow are as simple and as accurate as I could make them. Again, I have not documented them, because it is not my purpose here to prove that these things are contemporary LDS doctrine. And since your student has in some way made a prior decision to reject Mormonism in favor of Christianity, they are not intended for argumentation. If your student understood LDS doctrine on any point differently from the way I present it here, you have two options:

1. Let him explain what he thought he was taught and use your own research of Scripture to show him how it differs from truth, and/or

2. Document his doctrine for him using a standard Mormon doctrinal work (I recommend *Mormon Doctrine*, by

Bruce R. McConkie, because the way it is arranged makes it easy for a non-Mormon to access the information) or, less preferable, a comprehensive "anti-Mormon" book that footnotes and documents LDS doctrine.

You must not in any case compromise your influence with your student by squabbling over *today's* (not past) LDS doctrine and putting him in the position of having to defend it to you. Besides, the chances are very good that if one of you misunderstands Mormon doctrine, it is not the ex-Mormon.

The following list is a "menu" from which you can choose according to those areas in which your student has expressed problems in understanding. Of course, it is not comprehensive. This might also be the time to purchase *Mormons Answered Verse By Verse* by David Reed and John Farkas (Baker Book House, 1992) to give to your student or to help you with some questions that may arise about other verses.

Contrast

LDS: The Godhead consists of three persons, each of which is a god in his own right and is separate from the others in every way except in purpose. *Bible contrast: John 1:1, 14–18; 10:22–30; Hebrews 1:2–3; Acts 5:3–4; Psalm 139:7–10.*

LDS: God (the Father) is a resurrected being who achieved godhood by living obediently on another earth, under his god. *Bible contrast: Isaiah 43:10–11; 44:8; 45:21–22; 2 Samuel 7:22; Mark 12:32; Daniel 3:28; Jeremiah 10:10–12.*

LDS: Even Jesus taught a plurality of gods. *Bible contrast: John 10:34–35 along with 1 Corinthians 8:4–6; Mark 12:29–34.*

LDS: God (the Father) has a physical body of flesh and bones. *Bible contrast: John 4:24; 1 Kings 5:1–9; John 5:37.*

LDS: Bible passages like Exodus 31:18, Isaiah 30:27, and Isaiah 65:5 that mention physical body parts of God should be taken literally. *Bible contrast: 2 Chronicles 16:9; Psalm 91:4.*

LDS: The appearances of God to man in the past prove that he is a physical, not merely spiritual, being. *Bible contrast: Hebrews 11:27; Colossians 1:15; Deuteronomy 4:15–18; Exodus 24:9–11 (along with Acts 7:38); 1 John 4:12.*

LDS: Jesus is the literal son of God both in his spirit body and in his earthly body and was not conceived of the Holy Spirit, who is himself a separate being. *Bible contrast: Matthew 1:18.*

LDS: Since Jesus was created by God and has always been in subjection to God as a son, he has never been completely equal with God the Father. *Bible contrast: Hebrews 1:5; Philippians 2:5–11; Romans 9:5.*

LDS: There was a council in heaven in the preexistence where Jesus and Satan, both sons of God, gave advice on how to bring humans back to heaven. *Bible contrast: Romans 11:33–35.*

LDS: Since the Holy Ghost and Jesus both have spirit bodies of their own, they can only influence people, not dwell in them. *Bible contrast: Ephesians 3:14–19; John 14:23; Romans 8:9–11; 2 Corinthians 13:5; Colossians 1:27; Galatians 4:6.*

Symbolism

The subject of the oneness of God as expressed in the three Persons is perhaps the most difficult of all biblical concepts for an ex-Mormon to grasp (as if any of us can completely understand the limitless God). Giving up three very specifically defined, compartmentalized, visible gods in exchange for the admittedly incomprehensible Spirit Being of the Bible is a great sacrifice of thought for a Mormon. It is one of the great losses I have mentioned before.

The Bible is explicit in saying that the Father and Jesus are one, for instance; but there are few images or symbols that illustrate this or many other aspects of their being.

Here are my suggestions: Show your student the famous rallying cry of the Jewish nation in Deuteronomy 6:4 and point out that this transliterates to: "The LORD (Jehovah—singular) our God (Elohim—plural) is one LORD (Jehovah—singular)." Ask her to pray and meditate on this along with John 1:1 and ask God for insight into his nature and being.

Some biblical images do give us insight into the relationship between the elements of our God. John 14:5–14 should be read repeatedly and these things considered: In what way is Jesus the "way" to come to the Father if he is "in" the Father and the Father is "in" him? (Obviously, access to insight about this will not come from earthly logic. God alone can help the sincere seeker to know what this means.)

The most powerful images in the Bible compare God, a spirit, to equally intangible concepts like light and love. Is it possible, do you think, that God does not want to be quantified and analyzed, but has chosen instead to be known only by his words and actions in the Old Testament, by the embodiment of the Son in the New Testament, and by the influence of the Holy Spirit now?

In coming to earth, God put an opaque shell of a body over the submission aspect of himself. If you want to know how God thinks, how he acts, what angers him, what pleases him, look no further than the person of Jesus Christ. He is the only tangible symbol of God we will ever have.

Lesson 2

Redefining Salvation and the Church (Assessment)

Preparation

Pray together, asking God specifically to help you understand God better and to understand the biblical meaning of salvation and the church. Read again John 17:6–26.

Worldview Assumptions

If you were describing the church to someone from another culture, would you describe it more as an organization or as an entity? Why would you choose this aspect?

Who should make final decisions about doctrinal matters?

Should there be different "levels" of people in the church? If so, what should be the method of differentiating the strata?

What should be the criterion, if any, for choosing church leadership?

Can you know if a person is really a Christian? If so, how? If not, why not?

Are there circumstances under which someone should be excluded from fellowship in a local church?

Is humanity essentially good or essentially bad in nature?

What does it mean to be saved?

In salvation, who makes the first move, God or the individual?

What will heaven be like? Who will go to heaven?

What is hell like? Who will go to hell?

Can really good, sincere people be saved without knowing Jesus?

Epistemologies

What, in your experience, makes a church "work"?

When you were a child, what were you taught about the church? Did you see it more as a fellowship or as a constraint?

What images or analogies, if any, were used to explain the church to you as a teenager or as a young adult?

Can you remember any memorable lessons about the nature of the church, or did you learn more about it just from observing? If from observing, what stuck in your mind?

Does the idea of a paid ministry make you uncomfortable? Why or why not?

Were you ever taught a definition of the word *salvation*? If so, what was it?

Which was more significant to you growing up: learning the history of the Mormon Church or listening to testimonies from people who loved it?

Would you say that overall you had a good experience with the Mormon Church or a bad one? What do you base that assessment on?

Assignment for Home Study

Both you and the student should regularly ask God to openly share with you through his Word the truth about what salvation is and what the church is (the saved). Read at one sitting the Book of Ephesians at least three times before coming together again.

Redefining Salvation and the Church (Contrast and Symbolism)

Preparation

Before you come together to study, select the passages from the Book of Ephesians that most directly address the problem areas revealed in the student's responses of last week to the worldview and epistemology questions.

When you meet together, begin with prayer.

Then review the homework passages from the last lesson with the student, asking her which sections seemed most meaningful.

Ask if she has any questions.

Then read aloud from a Bible version other than the one the student used the sections you have selected beforehand.

Contrast

Again, using the conclusions you drew after reviewing the student's responses to the worldview and epistemologies questions of last week, select those elements from this section that seem to you to respond to the needs of your student.

LDS: There was a great apostasy, during which time the true church did not exist upon the earth. *Bible contrast: Matthew 16:13–18; Jude 24–25; John 17:11; 1 Corinthians 3:11.*

LDS: The church on earth must be headed by men with priesthood authority. *Bible contrast: Hebrews 4:14–5:10.*

LDS: The earthly leadership of the church must consist of a president and two counselors as well as twelve apostles. *Bible contrast: Ephesians 4:11–16; Colossians 1:15–20.*

LDS: You can know if a church is "true" by the way it is organized. *Bible contrast: John 8:31 with John 13:24–35.*

LDS: Church leaders should not be paid. *Bible contrast: 1 Timothy 5:17–18; 1 Corinthians 9:1–14.*

LDS: The rapid growth of the LDS church, even under persecution, proves that it is the true church. *Bible contrast: 2 Peter 2:1–2.*

LDS: The fact that there are so many Christian denominations on earth shows a need for divine revelation of which one is right. *Bible contrast: 1 Timothy 1:3–7; 6:3–16; 2 Timothy 3:12–17.*

LDS: To be saved you must be baptized by someone with priesthood authority and live all the laws and ordinances of the restored gospel. *Bible contrast: Romans 6.*

LDS: People are essentially noble beings who can exercise their free agency to decide if they want to become members of the church, and their obedience binds God to bless them. *Bible contrast: Ephesians 2:1–10.*

LDS: There are three degrees of heaven, and only faithful Mormons can go to the celestial kingdom. *Bible contrast: Read 1 Corinthians 15:35–49 in any version other than King James. Use a Greek-English aid to show meanings of the words celestial and terrestrial in the King James Version.*

LDS: Through baptism for the dead many people will accept the Mormon gospel, and almost all of humanity will spend eternity in one of the three degrees of heaven. *Bible contrast: Hebrews 9:27; 2 Corinthians 6:2; Matthew 7:13–14.*

LDS: Only Mormon apostates will go to hell. *Bible Contrast: Revelation 21:6–8; 22:14–15; 1 Corinthians 6:9–11; Ephesians 5:5.*

LDS: The "good fruit" of Mormonism—pure lives, good works, high standards, even miracles—prove that Mormonism is of God. *Bible contrast: Matthew 7:15–23; Isaiah 64:6.*

Symbolism

The Bible contains many symbols on the subject of the church. Here are Scripture passages to look up with the student and discuss: 1 Corinthians chapters 12–13; Ephesians 2:11–22; 2 Corinthians 3:2–3; 6:14–16; Ephesians 5:21–33. Be sure to be aware of any places here where the student sees echoes of Mormonism. Get him to define terms such as *prophet* with you, for example. Also, choose from among any of "the-kingdom-is-like" parables of Matthew or Luke and discuss what facet of the church is emphasized in them.

Above all, concentrate on the overall image and its implications.

Likewise, there are in Scripture some potent symbols of salvation. Read and discuss the following: Romans 6:1–14; 1 Corinthians 10:1–13; 15:33–58; Galatians 3:26–29; Colossians 2:9–15; Hebrews 10.

Again, the point must be made that in the absence of "formulas" in the Bible (for instance, to tell us everything we must do to be saved, or lists of all the characteristics of a true church) often we must let the Spirit teach us through the fifth epistemology. Do not neglect the symbols in favor of the contrasts.

Lesson 3

Redefining the Role of Scripture (Assessment)

Preparation

Pray with the student about the importance of God's communication with people through Scripture. Ask God specifically for the gift of insight into his Word's teaching about his Word. Ask if there are residual questions about last week's lesson, the study of the symbols about the church and salvation, or any other issues that have come up in personal Bible reading or study. Be ready also to share new insights you have received. Communicate to your student both information and your enthusiasm about studying God's Word (see Matt. 13:52).

Worldview Assumptions

Are people capable, do you think, of independently formulating moralities that will last?

Is it possible for a book written over two thousand years ago to address problems of modern society? Why or why not?

How would you define *inspiration?*

On what basis should a writing be considered inspired?

If a majority of people in a group (church or otherwise) decide that an action or an attitude is appropriate, should someone who disagrees just go along? If not, on what could such a person base a valid objection: personal likes and dislikes, example of others, traditions, something else?

Is it possible for a "regular person" to know whether or not a religious writing is from God? If so, how? If not, why not?

What percentage of the Bible, do you estimate, is actually understandable by the person of average intelligence?

Epistemologies

What was the first verse or passage from the Bible that you memorized?

When you were in the Mormon Church, how did you view the Bible as compared with the other standard works? As compared with conference talks?

Did you form an opinion about the relative importance of the Bible based on your reading it, hearing what leaders said about it, comparing its impact on doctrine to the other standard works, or the way you felt when you read it?

How did the Bible make you feel when you read it compared with when you read the other standard works or listened to leaders speak?

Assignment for Home Study

Read 2 Timothy 3:12–4:5 in at least three different Bible versions (provide the student access to versions she might not have). The student and you should pray this next week about the role of Scripture in your lives and memorize the four things for which the Timothy passage says Scripture is useful.

Redefining the Role of Scripture (Contrast and Symbolism)

Preparation

Review the homework passage from last week and ask if the student has any questions about it. Recite to each other the four uses of Scripture that the Timothy passage noted. Ask the student for an example of each, taken either from his own experience or from creating a hypothetical situation.

Contrast

LDS: The Bible could not be God's Word, because it contains a lot of contradictions. (Here the teacher must ask specifically which contradictions the ex-Mormon believes prove this point. Either be prepared to show how they are not contradictions or have access to a good supposed-Bible-discrepancies book such as mentioned in chapter 2 of this book.) *Bible contrast: John 17:17.*

LDS: The Bible is not complete, and there is evidence of parts that are missing, because it quotes from "lost books" such as the Book of Jashar mentioned in Joshua 10:13 and 2 Samuel 1:18. If these books that the Bible quotes are not in the Bible, that proves that it is incomplete. *Bible contrast: Acts 17:28; Titus 1:12.*

LDS: To know if a Scripture passage is from God, you should pray about it, and God will send you a "burning in the bosom" to prove to you if it is true. *Bible contrast: Proverbs 28:26; Jeremiah 17:9; Proverbs 16:25.*

LDS: The teachings of the living prophets are more important than older Scriptures because they reflect the Lord's more up-to-date concerns for us. These teachings can even supersede previous Scriptures or teachings of earlier prophets. *Bible contrast: Deuteronomy 18:18–22.*

LDS: The *Book of Mormon* teaches in 1 Nephi 13:24–28 that the Bible is unreliable because so much was taken out of it (in the Middle Ages when scribes were copying it). *Bible contrast: 1 Peter 1:23–25.*

LDS: Much of the "true gospel" that Jesus taught has been taken out of the Bible, so it was necessary for Joseph Smith to bring forth the *Book of Mormon* and subsequent teachings to restore the original, primitive gospel as Jesus taught it. *Bible contrast: Matthew 24:35.*

LDS: The *Book of Mormon* says in 1 Nephi 13:21 that the Bible is corrupted, can actually cause people to stumble, and lets Satan have power over such people. *Bible contrast: Ephesians 6:10–20; Psalm 119:97–104; John 15:1–8.*

Symbolism

Praise be to God, there are wonderful, powerful images in the Bible that show what our relationship with Scripture should be. Here are three, all of which should be explored in depth: Psalm 119:105; 2 Peter 1:16–21; Hebrews 4:12–13. The Psalms passage indicates the illuminating qualities of Scripture and its function as a reliable guide. The Peter passage deserves special attention because of its emphasis on the image of the "light shining in a dark place" and because of the way it shows the Spirit influenced Scripture writers.

The Hebrews passage is especially important for an ex-Mormon because of its indelible way of showing the pro-active role of God's Word—far from being the test case that our subjective feelings pass judgment on.

Lesson 4

Redefining Obedience and Trust in Others (Assessment)

Preparation

Pray together with the student, asking God that the student will learn to trust people again. Acknowledge the hurt that has resulted from his leaving Mormonism, and implore the help of Jesus, who surely felt the sting of betrayal in ways we will never know. Read aloud Hebrews 4:14–16.

Ask the student if he has residual questions about the role of Scripture. It is quite possible that at this point he will have some concern about the formation of the Christian canon. Of several excellent books on this subject, one that has been particularly helpful to me as an ex-Mormon (though it does not deal with LDS concepts per se) is F. F. Bruce's *The New Testament Documents: Are They Reliable?* (Eerdmans, 1959).

With your student's questions, you should always be prepared to say, "I may not know the answer to this question you've asked, but I'll do my best to find out." Your student will respect your honesty and thirst for knowledge more than any convincing bluffing that may crumble later.

Worldview Assumptions

The following questions may tap into some deep hurts and fears. Be prepared to do a lot of compassionate listening.

To what extent do you think leaders who mislead people in spiritual matters are responsible for their actions?

Are there some people whom God loves more than he loves others? How can you tell if a person is loved by God?

Who determines which rules of Christian conduct are the most important for you to follow?

Which is better, do you think: leaders who evaluate the abilities they see in their congregation and then assign tasks, or leaders who allow individuals to try to discover and employ their spiritual gifts for the congregation's good?

Will God evaluate or judge teachers and leaders differently than he does other Christians?

Is it either likely, or possible, or impossible to be a Christian without some sort of regular association with other Christians? Defend your answer.

How does someone balance law keeping and grace in the Christian life?

What should the word *submission* mean to a believer? Does it have limits? If so, what are they?

Epistemologies

When you were a Mormon, what did the word *obey* mean to you?

In what ways were the church's expectations of your conduct (dress, hair length, age to begin dating, other social behaviors) conveyed to you? Which was more important in helping you conform to your understanding of what the church expected: peer pressure, direct teaching, parental pressure, something other?

Did the church's clearly defined standards of conduct such as the Word of Wisdom help you or cause you to rebel?

Did you see yourself in any way as being on a "different plane" from the leaders you had? Give an example.

In your experience, on what basis were leaders of your local ward selected?

What were you taught in Sunday school, Mutual Improvement Association, priesthood meetings, Relief Society, etc., about a leader's ability to sin?

Did you as a Mormon believe that the prophet of the LDS church could lead his people astray? How did you come to this conclusion: on the basis of what you experienced, on the basis of what you were taught, or because of some sort of spiritual confirmation about him?

What penalties were you told about that would await someone who either fell away from the church or actually left it and taught against it? Was this just information you were taught, or did you see any such action being taken?

If someone referred to Mormonism as "an American religion," how would you respond?

Did you believe that your leaders in the Mormon Church could receive revelation for you? Could you receive revelation to guide them? On what did you base your beliefs in this matter—direct observation or teaching?

Assignment for Home Study

Make a contract commitment (write down and exchange your intentions) with your student to pray for insight on the nature of a Christian's obedience to his leaders. Read Acts 20:17–35 at least three times in the coming week. Make a list of all the characteristics of godly leadership that Paul addressed here (include his comments about himself as well). Pay special attention to details in verses 28–30.

Redefining Obedience and Trust in Others (Contrast and Symbolism)

Preparation

Pray for a spirit of love, not judgment, as you both look at the biblical concept of leadership. Exchange ideas from your repeated readings of the Acts 20 passage from the last lesson.

Read aloud Matthew 23:1–12. Emphasize that the difference between "obey them and do everything they tell you" and "do not do what they do" is based on two things: the truthfulness of what the teachers of the law and the Pharisees commanded (in this case, the commands were valid because they came from Scripture), and the integrity of their actions (which in this case were not valid, because they opposed God's commandments of loving one's neighbor as oneself). Do not go on until the student sees the difference here.

Contrast

LDS: Church leaders hold the priesthood, which is their ability to act in God's name and to represent him on earth. *Bible contrast: Hebrews 5:1.*

LDS: Church leaders can receive revelation for anyone over whom they are in authority, but a deacon cannot, for instance, receive revelation that contradicts or rebukes the prophet. *Bible contrast: 1 Timothy 5:19–20.*

LDS: The teachings of a living prophet always take precedence over those of the dead ones. *Bible contrast: Deuteronomy 18:21–22.*

LDS: If a man is ordained in the Melchizedek priesthood, he is called of God to that office and must be heeded. *Bible contrast: 1 Thessalonians 5:21, James 3:1–2; 1 John 4:1.*

LDS: The Lord would take a prophet of the church off the earth before he would allow him to lead the church astray. *Bible contrast: 1 Corinthians 10:1–12.*

LDS: There must be a prophet at the head of the latter-day church. *Bible contrast: Hebrews 1:1–2.*

LDS: Priesthood is a special calling only for those who will administer church ordinances. *Bible contrast: 1 Peter 2:4–10; Revelation 5:9–10.*

LDS: Inspired modern leaders can contradict prior doctrine. *Bible contrast: Galatians 1:6–9.*

Symbolism

Jesus used some powerful symbols to illustrate the concept of an individual's greatness to his disciples. The first, and quite surprising, symbol he used to illustrate greatness in the kingdom is found in Matthew 18:1–5. Surely few humans in this world wield any less extensive influence than a little child. And the humility Jesus spoke of is hardly one of the things they teach nowadays in "successful leadership" classes.

The second symbol of great leadership is found in John 13:1–17. Prayerfully consider its implications.

Continuing

By the time you have gone this far in teaching an ex-Mormon, the worldview and epistemology questions you have asked have undoubtedly caused other problem areas to surface.

That's not bad. It's great!

By teaching this precious new soul, you will save him or her from many lost hours—even days and years—of misconceptions and thus stunted spiritual growth.

I strongly advise you to use the same pattern in teaching on the new subjects, too. Pray about the subject matter, ask questions to determine worldview, establish your differing terminologies, and assess how the person learned the erroneous concept. Then use a concordance and/or any of the books on the following list of recommended reading to provide Bible verses to rub up against the preconception.

And please do not neglect symbolism. It may be hard work to uncover a biblical symbol, but the benefits for you both will far outweigh the effort.

It is my fervent prayer that God will abundantly bless your efforts.

Recommended Reading

Books on Mormon doctrine and history

The Changing World of Mormonism by Jerald and Sandra Tanner (Moody Press)

Where Does It Say That? by Bob Witte (Gospel Truths Ministry)

The Mormon Mirage by Latayne C. Scott (Zondervan)

Answering Mormons' Questions by Bill McKeever (Bethany House)

Mormons Answered Verse by Verse by David A. Reed and John R. Farkas (Baker)

Books on the experience of leaving Mormonism

Why We Left Mormonism: Eight People Tell Their Stories by Latayne C. Scott (Baker)

Books about worldview, logic, and associated subjects

The Universe Next Door by James W. Sire (IVP)

How To Read Slowly by James W. Sire (IVP)

Scripture Twisting by James W. Sire (IVP)

Come, Let Us Reason by Norman L. Geisler and Ronald M. Brooks (Baker)

Books about spiritual life and unseen realities

Knowing the Face of God by Tim Stafford (Zondervan)
Time and Eternity by Arthur Custance (Doorway Papers Series, Zondervan)
Fearfully and Wonderfully Made by Paul Brand and Philip Yancey (Zondervan)

Books about the Bible and Bible study

How to Read the Bible for All Its Worth by Gordon D. Fee and Douglas Stuart (Zondervan)
The New Testament Documents: Are They Reliable? by F. F. Bruce (Eerdmans)

Subject Index

Subject Index

139